PUBLIC LIBRARY

D0379198

PRAISE FOR A

"An NFL player becomes an All-Pro by relentlessly focusing on the fundamentals and executing them with sheer determination. The same is true to become an All Pro Dad. This book not only highlights the fundamentals of fatherhood, but also gives dads a winning game plan to do their most important job well."

—Tony Dungy, Super Bowl–winning
coach and NBC Sports commentator

"Leading a family is the hardest job a man can ever have. It is 24/7 leadership, teaching, modeling, forgiving, encouraging and loving—and there is always room for improvement. Mark Merrill has made a career out of teaching men how to raise their game as husbands and fathers, and his *All Pro Dad* lays out a solid game plan that will make a huge difference in your family."

—Dave Ramsey, New York Times best-selling
author and nationally syndicated radio show host

"What I count as the greatest success of my life is not what goes on when cameras are rolling during our NFL television broadcast, but rather in those private, loving moments with my family. Through *All Pro Dad*, Mark Merrill inspires fathers to be champions in their homes and equips them to love and lead their children well."

—James "JB" Brown, host of CBS's The NFL Today

"Just as every executive needs to understand his mission, strategies and responsibilities, every father needs to know those things as well. In this book, Mark Merrill lays out a clear fatherhood mission, strategic goals, and fine-tuned job description that will enable every dad to be a strong and respected leader in his home."

—Michael Ducker, COO and president,
International, FedEx Express

"Being a Heisman Trophy winner was a great honor, but being a dad is an even greater one. I want to live a life worthy of that honor by being an All Pro Dad to my kids. The seven essentials in Mark's book give us dads the tools we need to leave an enduring legacy of love for our kids."

—Danny Wuerffel, former NFL
quarterback and Heisman Trophy winner

"Chick-fil-A's success isn't just found in chicken sandwiches. It's found in the emotional connection we have with our customers. *All Pro Dad* provides a great recipe for men to really connect with their kids. I applaud Mark for the nuggets of wisdom he shares that will surely motivate dads to be the best they can be."

—S. Truett Cathy, founder and CEO of Chick-fil-A, Inc.

"As the important role of fathers in family life continues to be eroded by politically correct public commentary, it is refreshing to see a book like *All Pro Dad* that not only endorses fatherhood, but provides guidance for people who want to develop the kind of character in their children that will lead to successful lives and thriving societies."

—Benjamin S. Carson, Sr., M.D., Director of Pediatric Neurosurgery,
Johns Hopkins Hospital and author of Gifted Hands

"Leadership in business is important, but leadership in the home is even more critical. Mark Merrill pinpoints seven essentials that a father must know to be a loving leader in his home. *All Pro Dad* is a must-read book for the busy dad who is striving to be a hero to his kids."

—Wayne Huizenga, Jr., chairman, Rybovich
Marina and part owner of the Miami Dolphins

"When I was very young, my father said that the most important decisions I would ever make in life would start with the letter *M*: Master, Mate, and Mission. In *All Pro Dad*, Mark Merrill introduces seven essential *M*s for fathers to know as they strive to lead their families. I am honored and humbled to be a part of this crucial 'game-winning playbook' that is sure to strengthen families for generations to come."

—Dan T. Cathy, president and COO, Chick-fil-A, Inc.

"Every dad needs a game plan, training, and a great coach . . . *All Pro Dad* gives you all three. An inspired game plan that WILL help you win . . . effective training that has equipped thousands of men . . . and an experienced coach in Mark Merrill who will encourage you to do your very best. Read this book and then get 4 other fathers in the huddle with you who will challenge one another to become All Pro Dads!"

—*Dr. Dennis Rainey, host of FamilyLife Today*

"It is no surprise that our communities are experiencing many difficulties which can be attributed to the degradation of the family structure. We all realize there needs to be a change! The father plays a pivotal role in this endeavor because he must assume his position and develop a significant relationship with his children and reinvigorate the noble ideas of parental responsibility. This book will provide helpful anecdotes, narratives, and directives for dads who are searching for a new way to enrich the family unit."

—*Jim Caldwell, former head coach, Indianapolis Colts*

"I believe in the *All Pro Dad* principles, so anything Mark is associated with is excellent and worth your time."

—*Mark Richt, head coach, University of Georgia*

"In coaching, we are constantly trying to find ways to create, simplify, and practice fundamentals which provide an opportunity to be successful, knowing full well they will be tried and tested in the heat of battle. Mark's seven essentials in this book give us practical tools to sharpen our skills as fathers. These fundamentals are tried, tested, and proven in the arena of our homes."

—*Clyde Christensen, coach, Indianapolis Colts*

"I know how important it is for your fans to feel connected to you through your music. The more you speak to their hearts, the more you can inspire and bless them. It's also my job as a father. *All Pro Dad* is a must-read book that encourages me to connect, love, inspire, and bless those closest to me—my family."

—*Michael W. Smith, Grammy Award–winning recording artist*

"My father was a heavy drinker for many years and, unfortunately, I followed in his steps. Take it from me, I am excited about the practical 'God truths' that Mark Merrill shares in *All Pro Dad* that will help free men from their past and empower them into more godly, loving family relationships."

—*Norm Miller, chairman, Interstate Batteries*

"Being a great leader at the office takes hard work. Being a great dad in the home takes even more work. With *All Pro Dad*, Mark Merrill succinctly shares seven sound essentials that challenge us fathers to be the best we can be. Dads, whether your kids are young or old, this is a must-have book for you."

—*Jude Thompson, former CEO, Papa Johns*

"I know the importance of spending one-on-one time with each of my children. Mark Merrill gives me creative ideas on spending meaningful time with them and tips to build memories with my kids that will last a lifetime. This book is for every man who wants to be an All Pro Dad!"

—*Mark Dominik, general manager, Tampa Bay Buccaneers*

"Mark Merrill describes the power of an All Pro Dad. Imagine a world full of strong, loving fathers!"

—*Jeb Bush, former governor of the State of Florida*

ALL PRO DAD

Seven Essentials to Be a Hero to Your Kids

MARK MERRILL

THOMAS NELSON

Since 1798

NASHVILLE DALLAS MEXICO CITY RIO DE JANEIRO

To Megan, Emily, Hannah, Marky, and Grant.
How blessed I am to be your father.
I will always strive to be your All Pro Dad.
With all of my love, Dad.

© 2012 by Mark Merrill

All rights reserved. No portion of this book may be reproduced, stored in a retrieval system, or transmitted in any form or by any means—electronic, mechanical, photocopy, recording, scanning, or other—except for brief quotations in critical reviews or articles, without the prior written permission of the publisher.

Published in Nashville, Tennessee, by Thomas Nelson. Thomas Nelson is a registered trademark of Thomas Nelson, Inc.

Thomas Nelson, Inc., titles may be purchased in bulk for educational, business, fund-raising, or sales promotional use. For information, please e-mail SpecialMarkets@ThomasNelson.com.

Unless otherise noted, Scripture quotations are taken from the HOLY BIBLE, NEW INTERNATIONAL VERSION®, NIV®. Copyright ©1973, 1978, 1984, 2011 by Biblica, Inc.™ Used by permission of Zondervan. All rights reserved worldwide. www.zondervan.com.

Scripture quotations marked ESV are taken from THE ENGLISH STANDARD VERSION. Copyright © 2001 by Crossway Bibles, a division of Good News Publishers.

Library of Congress Cataloging-in-Publication Data

Merrill, Mark, 1958-
  All pro dad : seven fundamentals to be a hero to yourkids / Mark Merrill.
      p. cm.
  Includes bibliographical references (p.   ).
  ISBN 978-1-59555-507-6
  1. Parenting--Religious aspects--Christianity. 2. Fathers--Religious life. I. Title.
  BV4529.M45 2012
  248.8'421--dc23   2011048956

Printed in the United States of America
12 13 14 15 16 QG 6 5 4 3 2 1

CONTENTS

Contents

FOREWORD BY TONY DUNGY

I met Mark Merrill in 1997, a year after I had become the head coach of the Tampa Bay Buccaneers. Mark was president of a national organization based in Tampa called Family First and, at the time, some of my assistant coaches and I were looking for help. We were trying to balance the demands of our job with our desire to be good husbands and fathers. We were told Mark may have some ideas that could help us.

That meeting was the beginning of a wonderful relationship, and I did get some excellent parenting tips and suggestions from Mark. The more we talked, though, the more I discovered that I wasn't alone in my parenting struggles. A lot of men, from all walks of life, were facing many of the same issues. As Mark and I continued to talk, we thought that we might be able to utilize the popularity of football to help men in their quests to be great dads. That's how the concept of All Pro Dad started, and it has blossomed into a support system for men all over the country.

Over the past fourteen years, Mark has used the platform of the All Pro Dad program to help men in a number of ways. The program has daily e-mails, monthly school-based breakfasts, and large events in NFL stadiums across the United States that teach men the fundamentals of fatherhood, show them creative ways to spend time with their children, and encourage them to celebrate the joys of parenting. Now, with the release of *All Pro Dad: Seven Essentials to Be a Hero to Your Kids*, Mark is putting this practical information into one playbook for men.

In our country today, there is a tremendous need for this information. Some men have had the benefit of having a great father who was able to show them how to effectively nurture their children. I did, and I consider myself very fortunate to have learned so many things from my dad. Others of us have not been so blessed. You may not have had a father you want to emulate, or may not have grown up with a dad in your home at all. But whatever your background, when you have children of your own, you realize that you will only have one chance to raise them, with no opportunity to try it again if it doesn't go well.

Being a father is a demanding job and all the signs tell us that we are not doing a great job in this country. We're all aware of the statistics regarding families in America. The staggering increases in our divorce, high school dropout, and teen crime rates all suggest our family structure is breaking down. What responsibility do we, as men, have for this? And more importantly, how do we correct the problem?

I believe that's the real beauty of this book. It not only looks at the responsibilities that men have to develop our families and parent our children wisely, but it also goes into detail on *how* to do it well. And these aren't merely theoretical suggestions but sound, biblical principles on fatherhood that have stood the test of time.

The All Pro Dad blueprint breaks down into two fundamental principles—love and leadership. This book talks about these two concepts from God's perspective, which may be very different from the way we've looked at them in the past. And this book shows how we need to apply that biblical love and leadership in our homes.

When examining God's definition of love, you see that it's not merely an emotional response to your wife or your kids. God's love is putting their well-being first and doing everything you can to make their lives full and complete. The idea of leadership is really not that much different. It means putting the welfare of the group above all else, with the leader paving the way and making decisions for the benefit of the group, and not just himself.

Using those two principles as the basis for parenting will cause you to look at the job in a completely different way. It will cause you to ask yourself some questions about your life: Why am I here? And what's my real purpose in life? And if that purpose is to help build up your children, help them grow with the best chance to be successful in life, and leave a legacy that goes beyond your own accomplishments, then this book is for you. I hope you will read it, digest it, and use it not only as food for thought but also as food for action. Put these principles into practice and they will definitely help you become an All Pro Dad!

INTRODUCTION

Why the Quest?

We reached our destination. The majestic, mountainous towers that seemed to reach as high as heaven—the Towers of Paine—had been conquered. It was twenty-two years ago, just a few months before my wedding, that a friend and I trekked through Patagonia. The twelve-day excursion was a magnificent, but rigorous, adventure through peaks, glaciers, and rivers in this southern portion of the Andes mountain range in South America. It involved some tough climbing and very narrow trails where one misstep could cause a quick departure from our time here on earth. But the payoff for our difficult hike was immeasurable.

During my twenty-one-year quest of being a dad, I've experienced the joy of standing on mountaintops and the pain of crawling through valleys. Tailwinds have carried me forward, and headwinds have slowed me down. Fatherhood is full of fun, excitement, and adventure, but difficulty and pain in raising children may unexpectedly leap across our trail like a wild beast attacking us and our kids. When they do, we need to slay them, push them off our path, and press on. Our job as dads is to stay the course and to persevere when trouble comes our way, even during the darkest and most difficult hours of our children's lives.

Like you, I'm struggling. I'm struggling on my journey as a father and through this thing we call life. I've never felt completely at home anywhere—any house that I've lived in, any office I've worked in, or any church I've worshipped at. I kind of sense that there just isn't a place where I really belong. Instead, I feel like a foreigner from another country, a citizen of another land. Why? Well, maybe it's because I am. I'm not meant to be here forever. I'm here for just a relatively short time.

I'll be going to my eternal home soon. Will it be today? Maybe. Next year? Perhaps. Thirty or forty years from now? I can't answer that question. But I do know that with each day that passes, the probabilities increase. And I also know that I want whatever time I have on this earth to matter. I want it to matter for God, for Susan, my wife of twenty-two years, and for my five children—Megan, Emily, Hannah, Mark Jr., and Grant. I want whatever influence I have as a man and father to last for generations, and hopefully, forever.

My guess is you do too. And I know your time is valuable, so I want to assure you, if you take the energy to hike the path I prescribe in the coming chapters, you and your family will change. It is my hope that your return on investment will be enormous, not because I'm a pillar of wisdom, but because the truths we'll mine are eternal and life changing. So as we walk side by side, you and I will explore our hearts and minds and perhaps discover some very crucial things about ourselves, which will enrich our lives and the lives of our children. We'll learn the fatherhood fundamentals and explore the 7 essential Ms that will enable us to execute those fundamentals well. The 7 Ms will also motivate and equip us to be the kind of dads we were created to be and, as a result, a hero to our kids.

During our time together, you'll also get to know remarkable leaders and fathers who are striving to be the best fathers they can be. They're people you may know—executives and CEOs of major corporations, like Truett Cathy, founder of Chick-fil-A; Michael Ducker, COO and President, International, FedEx Express; Norm Miller, founder of Interstate Batteries; J. Wayne Huizenga Jr., chairman of Rybovich Marina and part owner of the Miami Dolphins; and Jeb Bush, former governor of Florida and businessman. NFL coaches, sports leaders, and celebrities, including Super Bowl–winning head coach and NBC commentator Tony Dungy; host of CBS's *The NFL Today* James "JB" Brown; Tampa Bay Buccaneers general manager Mark Dominik; and Grammy Award–winning recording artist Michael W. Smith will also share their stories and help us make each moment of this journey count. And they will encourage you because, like all of us, they have had their share of failure, discouragement, and headwinds. Still, when the headwinds may have been strong enough to knock them off their paths, their desire to live lives that matter prevailed.

My hope is that the words on these pages will press against your back and will be like a tailwind for you, gently propelling you forward to a meaningful and fulfilling life as a father. I think it's going to be an amazing adventure. I'm ready to go. How about you? We may be starting at the foot of the mountain, but we will see the summit soon. When we do, I hope you'll witness the awesome, breathtaking view as a dad who has a new vision for his life and the lives of his children. Let's take the first step.

1

FATHERHOOD FUNDAMENTALS

Champions are champions not because they do anything extraordinary but because they do the ordinary things better than anyone else.

—Chuck Noll, former head coach of the Pittsburgh Steelers and four-time Super Bowl winner

G entlemen, this is a football." With those five famous words, legendary NFL football coach Vince Lombardi communicated his point to his players each year at the beginning of the Green Bay Packers training camp. With pigskin held high in the air, he was telling his team that they must always start with the fundamentals.

"I can remember my first team meeting ever in the National Football League," Super Bowl–winning player and coach Tony Dungy shared with me as he reminisced about his days playing for the Pittsburgh Steelers. "I was a rookie. Chuck Noll was the coach and the Steelers had won two Super Bowls already. And I thought I was going to hear some fantastic stuff describing how you get to be Super Bowl champions; how you get to be a great player.

"Coach Noll—I'll never forget it—said, 'Champions are champions not because they do anything extraordinary but because they do the ordinary things better than anyone else.' What he was saying was, you've got this misconception that you've gotta do these spectacular highlight-reel type things, you've gotta have special gifts and special talents to be a Super Bowl winner or an All-Pro. He said, no, that's not it. There are fundamentals that it takes to play the game. Executing those fundamentals, not forgetting them, and executing them day in and day out, that's how you become great. That's how you win. That's how you become an All-Pro. And he was right."[1]

Just as knowing and executing the fundamentals of football are key to a player becoming an All-Pro, knowing and executing the fundamentals of fatherhood better and more consistently than everyone else are key to a father becoming an All Pro Dad. Many books, blogs, and seminars do a good job listing things men should say and not say, do and not do as fathers. Men need lists, and lists are good. But we can't skip the fundamentals. And the two most important fundamentals of fatherhood are love and leadership. Before you think I'm getting soft by talking about love, you need to know that love is anything but soft. It's strong. James "JB" Brown, host of *The NFL Today*, is a big man with a big heart. During one of our visits, JB shared with me that "People think love is soft and weak, but it is really a sign of strength."[2] It's strong. It's powerful. It's courageous.

What drives a fireman to put on a fifty-pound tank and climb the stairs of the World Trade Center? What inspires a G.I. to storm Omaha Beach under a cloud of enemy gunfire? As author G. K. Chesterton wrote, "The true soldier fights not because he hates what is in front of him, but because he loves what is behind him."[3] Love for others is what makes a man a man. And a man's love, his manhood, starts with what is right behind him—his family.

So in this chapter, we'll focus on the fatherhood fundamentals of love and leadership. We're going to learn what they really are and why they are so important for fathers. In the next seven chapters we'll tackle the "7 Ms" that are essential for every man to know to effectively execute those fundamentals—Makeup, Mind-set, Motive, Method, Model, Message, and Master. Every father must know these 7 Ms to expand his capacity to love and, in turn, lead his children well.

THE FIRST FUNDAMENTAL—LOVE

"Truly, truly, truly love. That's the most powerful thing there is." Those are the words spoken by UCLA's legendary basketball coach John Wooden, at the age of ninety-nine shortly before his death.[4] Love's power is apparent. But its essence can be tough to grasp. Bookstores and shelves in homes are filled with books on what love is, how to love, what love does and does not do. Unfortunately, many miss the real mark of love.

If you asked ten adults what love is, you'd probably get ten different answers. Love is tough to define. Coach Wooden went on to say, "The most important word in our language is 'love.'" *Love* is the greatest word with the greatest value and the greatest power in the world. The Roman poet Virgil said, "Love conquers all things."[5] The great Russian novelist Leo Tolstoy said, "All, everything that I understand, I understand only because I love."[6] And the political leader of India, Mahatma Gandhi, said, "There only is life where there is love. Life without love is death."[7]

The Author of Wisdom clearly tells us that love is the greatest. When the cunning Pharisees asked Jesus of Nazareth, "Teacher, which is the greatest commandment in the Law?" Jesus replied: "'Love the Lord your God with all your heart and with all your soul and with all your mind.' This is the first and greatest commandment. And the second is like it: 'Love your neighbor as yourself.'"[8]

Okay, if you still don't believe love is the most important thing, just go and ask someone who has never really been loved.

Myths and Misunderstandings About Love

Love is the greatest, but it is also undoubtedly the most overused and underused, misapplied and misunderstood word in the English language. It is overused and misapplied with reckless abandon on most television shows and commercials you watch. Remember the "I love you, man" beer commercial? For decades, musicians such as the Beatles have made love their hallmark—"She loves you, yeah, yeah, yeah." The books you read and websites and blogs you look at talk about love as well. It's so apparent, examples are probably unnecessary. But I don't want you to think that it's mostly bad. I like a lot of those shows and songs. I'm just trying to make the point that we use this amazing word without even thinking about it. As a result, we perpetuate myths about its meaning.

Love is also underused and misconstrued in word and deed by husbands, wives, parents, children, grandparents, grandchildren, relatives, friends, and coworkers. Loving others doesn't mean liking. We can love others without having to like what they do. My wife, Susan, and I, especially when we're having a disagreement, will sometimes say to each other, "I love you. But I sure don't like you right now." What we're really saying is, "I love you no matter what, but I don't like the way you are acting right now."

We apply the word *love* when we speak of things as well. We say, "I love my car." "I love their french fries." "I love that dress." Sure, those things may be appealing and pleasing to one of our five senses—sight, hearing, taste, touch, smell—but it is not the right application of our love. We weren't designed to love inanimate objects. Objects are not capable of receiving and giving love; only people are. If we attempt to "love" things, then, more often than not, we'll use people and end up with shallow relationships, meaningless stuff, and no one to share it with. But if you and I love people, and use things for their intended purpose, we'll have rich relationships and lasting joy in life.

The Risks of Love

Be aware. We may invest a lot of personal time and emotional capital in our spouses or children and not see any kind of ROI—return on investment. But, as we'll soon see, that's what love is all about—investing with no expectation of return. Having said that, we need to remember that all loving involves some risk. Author C. S. Lewis observed:

> To love at all is to be vulnerable. Love anything, and your heart will certainly be wrung and possibly be broken. If you want to make sure of keeping it intact, you must give your heart to no one, not even to an animal. Wrap it carefully round with hobbies and little luxuries; avoid all entanglements; lock it up safe in the casket or coffin of your selfishness. But in that casket— safe, dark, motionless, airless—it will change. It will not be broken; it will become unbreakable, impenetrable, irredeemable.[9]

Genuine Love

Do you know how U.S. Secret Service agents determine if money is counterfeit? They don't start by studying counterfeit currency. They start with the real thing. They learn that genuine currency has a texture of raised ink; sharp, fine printing; red and blue color strands; a watermark; serial numbers; and other security features. When they know the real thing, they can easily spot a fake. As we saw earlier, there is a lot of counterfeit love talk in our world today. The best way to spot it? We've got to study the real thing. So let's get to it.

While searching for this Holy Grail definition, you need to know something right up front. Thousands of people over the course of thousands of years have worked to define the word *love*. There are as many definitions out there as there are grains of sand on the beach. I shared just a few of them with you earlier. Although I've spent a lot of time researching definitions of love, I'm not going to rehash all of those definitions. I've done the work for you, so let me give it my best shot. You ready? Here is the treasured definition: God is love. That's it. But I know that definition may not satisfy your curiosity, so let's continue to study the genuine nature of love. As we do, please remember that I just gave you the best and most genuine definition of love you'll ever find and nothing else will ever match it.

Picture in your mind a wedding at a church. The young bride and groom are on the altar facing each other, hand in hand. Their sparkling eyes and glowing faces complement the flowing wedding gown and tux. The pastor stands before the excited and hopeful couple and says with confidence, "Love is patient when you *feel* like being patient, love is kind when you *feel* like being kind . . ." Right? Of course not. He says, "Love is patient, love is kind. It does not envy, it does not boast, it is not proud. It is not rude, it is not self-seeking, it is not easily angered, it keeps no record of wrongs. Love does not delight in evil but rejoices with the truth. It always protects, always trusts, always hopes, always perseveres."[10]

In doing so, what is he really saying about love? He's saying love is not just a feeling; it is a decision. Love does not say, "Feel this way." Love says, "Act this way." Love is an act of the will to be patient, kind, gentle, humble, sincere, compassionate, giving, faithful and trusting, forgiving, uniting, and persevering. Love is all about serving and giving selflessly and sacrificially to another person. The best way to spell love? G-I-V-E. It's looking not only to your own interests but also to the interests of others. It's doing what's best for others no matter what it costs you personally.

Love says, "I want what's best for you! That is why I'm talking to you about this, that is why I'm doing this, that is why I'm making this decision."

Love says, "No longer will I live my life for me. I will think about self less and you more."

Love says, "I'm choosing to be at my best even when you're not at your best."

Love says, "What I want isn't important, but what you want is paramount."

The Unconditional Nature of Love

As a real estate attorney, I drafted many contracts. In every valid contract there is something called "consideration." Consideration is when you give something knowing you will get something else in return. It's conditional. It's an "if I do this, then you'll do that" kind of thing. But love is unconditional. Love is not a transaction; it's an action. Love is not reciprocal; it's sacrificial.

"So, are you doing this?" my wife, Susan, asked me as we sat on the couch after she had just read the first draft for this chapter.

"Doing what?" I responded.

"Are you exercising this fundamental of love, unconditional love, with our children?" she continued.

I really thought it was an off-base question. "Yes, of course I am. I'm constantly telling them that I love them no matter what, and they know I love them unconditionally."

Susan then dug deeper in, saying, "I know you say that a lot and really mean it, but do your facial expressions, tone of voice, and actions always show it? Think about Marky. Sometimes your looks of disapproval for what he did or didn't do, or not being excited about something he is doing might send the opposite message to him." Susan then went on to give me a couple examples of this.

It was a full body slam as I had never thought about it that way. And it hurt. But I thanked Susan and stopped writing for the day as I pondered what she said. I then determined in my mind that I was going to really work on this fundamental. I need to show unconditional love not only with my words, but also with my tone of voice and facial expressions. I've got to get this right!

Grammy Award–winning recording artist Michael W. Smith, father of five and grandfather of five, is a living testimony to the fact that love is never wasted and must be unconditional. "I'm a perfect example of a guy who had amazing parents—still do, they're my biggest fans," Michael shared with me. He then paused as his mind went back many years ago. "But, you know, I started playing with the fire— alcohol and drugs. I didn't think I could get burned. And for four years, I was a mess. I mean, I was a complete mess. I almost died a few times. It's crazy."

Michael then seemed to say with a great sense of gratitude, "And I'm convinced to this day that part of my rescue was my mom and dad loving me unconditionally, even knowing everything that I was doing. They just loved me. It was unconditional love and they were on their knees for me, especially in my crazy party days here in Nashville. And I think that's what you gotta do as a father if your kids have wandered. The best thing you can do for them is just love them and pray for them."[11] Michael's parents' love for him was not reciprocal during those years; it was sacrificial.

Love in Action

As I sat with the popular former governor, now businessman, Jeb Bush, in his modest Coral Gables, Florida, office, he paused from his busy workday to reflect upon his life. He thoughtfully shared these intimate thoughts with me, which I pass along to you. "We all have loving thoughts, but if they remain passive, they're completely useless because they don't nourish anything. They can actually create resentment. Converting those thoughts into action shouldn't take half a lifetime, but in my case, it has. But I've noticed I'm getting better at loving. I look back at my life and realize things are not as complicated as I thought. Why does it take a half-a-lifetime experience to get to the simple things?"[12] Love is not passive; it is an action. It's something we must demonstrate day in and day out, even when everything inside of us screams, "No, that person did me wrong, they don't deserve it!"

Let me give you an example:

"Hello, Mr. Merrill? This is John Johnson from Tampa Fire and Rescue. Do you know what's happened to your home?"

"No," I said into the phone with a questioning tone.

"Well, you have a major problem in your home. It's flooded," he added.

"What?" I gasped. "What happened?"

"I would just suggest you get here quickly," he exclaimed.

"Thank you," I said hurriedly as I hung up the phone. I jumped into my car and raced home from the office in the pelting Florida rain. Once I pulled into the driveway, I realized what had happened. We were getting a new roof on our historic old house and the workers had taken off the old one but, for whatever reason, they were not able to get a tarp secured to cover the house. So, in came the heavy rain. The attic, second floor, and first floor were all inundated. Beautiful old plaster ceilings fell to the floor, antique furniture was ruined, and clothes were soaked. That night, June 1, 2011, we moved out.

Sure, it's tough for my family to be houseless. You get kind of disoriented and feel as though you're in a fog. But we're not homeless. We know where our permanent home really is. And nobody was injured. So basically it was just stuff that was destroyed. Stuff that can be replaced or wasn't really needed.

Over the course of the next few days after the flood, we had to do many things, including finding a place to stay for the next eight to twelve months while our home was being rebuilt. But as I thought about it, I determined that the most important thing I needed to do was to be a good example to all the people I would have to deal with through the process—the insurance companies, the adjusters, the contractors, the cleaners, and so on.

This incident, which occurred right in the middle of writing this book, would test my resolve. Would I just write about love? Or, would I really live it out? Well, I can tell you that I've failed in some ways, especially in the area of patience, but I'm grateful that I've been given opportunities to increase my capacity to love and demonstrate love to others despite my failures.

After I wrote about what we went through on my blog, to my surprise, our roofer posted a comment on my site. It was a great encouragement to me in light of the struggles we faced. "Never have I seen or experienced such a magnitude of water in a home before, and hope never to see it again," commented the roofer.

On the same note never have I seen an action such as I witnessed from owners whose home had water dripping from every ceiling in the house. As I entered the home, I braced myself knowing that the typical owner would be down into my face yelling, cursing, and threatening me. Instead I witnessed owners, obviously in shock and disbelief, but also providing me a sense of grace in the midst of chaos. There was a difference in their reaction that made them non-typical owners for the situation.

Love is an action and we must choose to show it to others even when we think they don't deserve it.

So the first fundamental of fatherhood is love. You can't lead your family effectively without it. First love, then lead.

The Second Fundamental—Leadership

For several generations our world has taught us that mind and strength, mental and physical, are for work; heart and soul, emotional and spiritual, are for home. For instance, we talk about leadership in the context of business and business relationships and talk about love in the context of home and personal relationships.

Think about it. How many business seminars on love have you attended, or how many books on home leadership have you read? But love is the essential thing in all areas of life. And leadership must be recognized as extremely important not only in work but also in the home. In fact, Jim Caldwell, former head coach of the Indianapolis Colts, believes the home is the incubator of leadership. He told me, "Leadership is first developed in the home."[13]

J. Wayne Huizenga Jr., chairman of Rybovich Marina and part owner of the Miami Dolphins, shared with me his thoughts on love and leadership: "We don't talk a lot about leadership in the home and not much has been written about leadership in the home. Nobody really trains us to be leaders at home like they do at work." Wayne paused and then went on to say: "It's so much more difficult to lead at home than it is at work because at work, the motive is your getting a paycheck and if it doesn't work out, we can separate. But at home, we're not getting a paycheck and we can't separate. They're your family, regardless."[14]

Wayne is on target. Leading at home can be one of the toughest places to lead. You can't fire your child. There is no paid time off. There are no raises or bonuses. The rewards are rarely immediate or apparent. How many times have you received a standing ovation when you walked in the door, or gotten the father-of-the-year award to put in your trophy case? But, as we'll see later on, a dad will ultimately find joy and fulfillment as he strives to be an All Pro Dad.

Leading at home is also tough because we have to discipline our kids. But a loving and leading father must discipline his children. I've often said to each of my five children, "I love you. And I'm only saying or doing this because it's what's best for you."

Every once in a while one of them will challenge me on it.

"How is taking away my cell phone in my best interest?" my son, Marky, asked after we took away his privilege of using it because he was speaking disrespectfully to us.

"Well, having a cell phone is a privilege so that you can communicate with your friends. When you communicate respectfully with us then you get to keep that privilege. When you don't, you lose it. So not having your phone for a while will remind you of the importance of talking respectfully to us."

Do I like to discipline? No. Does my son like it? Of course not. But, if I really do it in the right way and for the right reasons, he will at least know that I'm doing it out of love and, as a result, I'll earn the right to lead him in other areas of life too.

You Are a Leader and a Follower

So, are you a leader? A leader is a person who has followers. If someone is following you, then you are influencing that person. That is, you are effecting change in that person. The change may be in speech, behavior, or action. Therefore, at its core, leadership is influence.

Are you a dad, mom, husband, wife, grandparent, relative, employer, employee, or friend? If so, then you are a leader. You are also a follower. Great leaders are great followers. Each and every one of us is a leader and a follower. Each and every one of us is influencing and being influenced. We are all leading sometimes and being led at other times. For instance, in earlier years, as our kids were getting ready for school, Susan was the influencer and our children were the influenced. She decided what they would eat and wear, and they followed. Our children then went to school and became the influencer in certain situations with their peers who followed. Then the bell rang and the teacher had all the influence, and our children once again became the ones influenced, and so on.

In every situation where you are in the presence of one or more other people, there is a dominant influencer. Susan and I are constantly asking our teens, especially if they aren't having a good attitude after being with certain friends, "Are you influencing your friends more than they are influencing you?" That's because we want them to recognize that in every relationship, one person is, in small or big ways, more dominant in their influence and can impact the behavior of others. We want our kids to either be the influencer, the leader, or be influenced in a positive way as a follower.

Many fathers have excelled at leading their team at work but have fumbled the ball in the area of home leadership. Now, it's not necessarily because they haven't tried. As I'll address in the chapter on Mind-set, there are a number of factors that have influenced a father's ability to lead effectively in the home. I confess I've dropped the ball and made plenty of mistakes as a husband, father, son, brother, and friend. But anyone who knows me knows that I always want to learn, to be better and do better. Connecting love and leadership is key in us moving the ball forward as fathers.

THE LOVE AND LEADERSHIP CONNECTION

What's love got to do with leadership? Everything. Love is leadership's unseen essential. We don't see it and it's not normally talked about in the context of leadership, but it's a vital component in the life of every great leader.

Herb Kelleher, former CEO of Southwest Airlines, said, "I would far rather have a business led by love than by fear." So, if you include yourself among those who find "love" a hard word to link with "leadership," then remember this: Herb Kelleher's Southwest Airlines, the company he declared from the start to be "led by love," whose headquarters is called "Love Airfield" and whose stock market listing is "LUV," is the most profitable airline in U.S. commercial aviation history.[15]

Love is one of the most effective and efficient leadership strategies that ever existed. And infusing love into an organization, as well as the home, delivers a better ROI than any other single investment you can make. Great organizations and great families are fueled by loving leaders.

In my conversation with JB Brown, host of *The NFL Today*, he further commented that "true love is to be displayed consistently in all settings. When it is manifested in one's behavior in the workplace and at home, success often follows. Love is key in leadership."[16] Michael Ducker, COO and President, International, FedEx Express, punctuated what JB said. "As a leader, I am compelled to love all people under my care, my employees and my family." Mike went on to tell me that "life is more about relationships than anything else. A part of those relationships, on the job and in the home, is knowing people personally and caring about their lives. If your employees know they have a boss that knows and cares about them, they are more inclined to follow you as a leader. The same holds true for our children."[17]

EXPANDING OUR CAPACITY TO LOVE AND LEAD

We are all born with the ability to love, but we must expand our capacity to love. Now here's the key point I want you to remember: our capacity to love will determine our capacity to lead at home, at work, and in life. In other words, when we genuinely love our spouse, our children, and others, when they know we want what's best for them, they'll follow us. They'll say to themselves: "You've loved me. You've earned the right to lead me. I'll follow you." Your leadership of your family will grow in direct proportion to the love that you show your family.

The way we increase our love capacity is counterintuitive. Normally, capacity increases when *something is filled*. But our capacity to love is increased the most when *someone is emptied*. Our capacity to love expands when we empty ourselves and give of ourselves to others. As fathers, we must show love to grow love. The more love you show, the more your capacity to love will grow.

For a last will and testament to be effective and the inheritance to be passed on, a person must die. For our leadership of our family to be effective and an inheritance of a loving dad to be passed on to our children, we must die to our self-focused ways. That may mean that we do things in an uncommon way. For example, we might work fewer hours at the office when our children are growing up so we can spend more time with them, and then work more when they're grown. Or, it might even mean foregoing that promotion that would have required us to move or work longer hours. It might mean delaying things we'd like to do or interests we'd like to pursue.

Many years ago and throughout my years of practicing law, I had a desire to serve in public office. Subsequently, I had the opportunity to run for Congress. After doing some real soul-searching and discussing it with Susan, I determined that I was not willing to sacrifice the time with my family to do it. The decision was made and I've never looked back.

Our capacity to love will expand exponentially as we die to self. And as we expand our capacity to love, we'll also expand our capacity to lead. Can a leader "get by" without loving? Sure, but leadership – love = limited leadership— limited in breadth and depth. Leadership + love = lasting leadership. Those who grow the most in life's fundamental— love—will grow to be the greatest leaders at home, at work, and in life.

THE 7 MS

"In 2008, my last year coaching with the Colts, we had drafted Anthony Gonzalez," Tony Dungy started.

He wasn't able to come to work out with us in the spring because he was still in school. He was at Ohio State and not graduating until June, so he was going to miss all the May and June workouts. And Peyton Manning, by then, was in his eleventh year. He'd been MVP of the league three times already. You know, he was really at the pinnacle of his career. That spring, he would get in his car twice a week and drive to Columbus, Ohio. Drive three hours over, spend an hour and a half with Anthony, throw him the ball, run routes, spend half an hour with him going over the playbook, and then drive three hours back. So, he was taking seven and a half hours out of his day twice a week to make sure that Anthony Gonzalez got caught up and was prepared when the training camp started. That's the kind of dedication people don't always see.

When people ask me what makes Peyton Manning special, he's gifted, he is talented, he's got the physical tools you need. He had the background and all that from watching his dad and going to the University of Tennessee. But the thing that separates him from everybody else is that dedication and that work ethic and that desire to do whatever it takes to not only get himself ready, but to get his teammates ready to play well. That's why he's an All-Pro.

Tony added, "So being an All-Pro in the NFL takes a little bit of talent; but more than anything else, it takes hard work, it takes dedication, and it takes teamwork. And if any of those are missing, it really becomes difficult. Also, an All-Pro is a guy who is very consistent. He does it week in and week out. He plays at that high level all the time."[18] And an All-Pro at the NFL level is someone who, like Peyton Manning, has studied his playbook day in and day out, watched hundreds of hours of game film, practiced what he's learned, and executed the fundamentals heroically on the field with sheer determination.

Well, to become an All Pro Dad, those same principles apply. An All Pro Dad is no ordinary dad. He not only knows the fundamentals but also does whatever it takes to execute them like nobody else. All Pro Dads are All Pro Dads "not because they do anything extraordinary but because they do the ordinary things better than anyone else."

Hail Mary passes don't work in fatherhood. Fathering is all about a dad moving the ball forward in his relationship with his child, one yard at a time, day in and day out. At the same time, avoiding major, costly mistakes and turnovers are critical as a man executes his fatherhood game plan. Men who really want to be the best dads they can be—to be All Pro Dads—must study, watch, practice, and ultimately execute the fundamentals of fatherhood—love and leadership—with great purpose and perseverance.

To effectively execute those fundamentals, every father must know these 7 Ms—Makeup, Mind-set, Motive, Method, Model, Message, and Master. Then, and only then, will he be able to expand his capacity to love and, in turn, expand his capacity to lead his children.

In the next seven chapters as we explore these essential 7 Ms, we'll dig deep to answer some critical questions that will enable us to work toward our goal of becoming an All Pro Dad. The first question we'll answer in chapter 2 is: *Who am I?* When we answer this, we'll know our Makeup—our identity and gifts. As we move the ball down the field in chapter 3, we'll be challenged to have a new Mind-set as a father. We'll be handed a new job description and game plan as we consider the question: *What's my purpose?* In chapter 4, we'll discover the answer to: *Why do I do what I do?* That answer will determine our Motive. Then I'll share ideas in chapter 5 that will provide us with a practical Method to love and lead our families—*How can I better love my family?* In chapter 6, we'll see that each and every father must also know he is a Model. There, we'll address: *What should I model to my children?* Then we'll discuss knowing our Message in chapter 7. There, we'll consider the question: *What do I need to share with others?* As we move toward our goal of becoming an All Pro Dad, we'll go deep in chapter 8 as we answer: *Who or what am I living for?* When we answer this, we'll know our Master.

It is my hope that when you make these 7 Ms your play-book, you will become a loving leader in your home, you will be a hero in your child's eyes, and you will enjoy renewed and flourishing relationships with your family.

HUDDLE UP AND ASK YOUR CHILD:

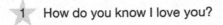

1   How do you know I love you?

2   How should someone act when they love you?

3   Should you love people who don't love you back? Why or why not?

4   Who is the greatest leader you know? Why did you choose him or her?

5   What is one thing I can do to better lead our family?

2

KNOW YOUR MAKEUP

Who Am I?

Know thyself.

—Plato

Yulia was a little girl who lived in the small town of Kansk in Siberia, Russia. She was born out of wedlock to a mother who was too young to care for her and who drank way too much vodka. Her father was also consumed with alcoholism, and one day, when Yulia was still a little girl, he was found frozen to death next to their hut. Now all alone, she went to live with her elderly grandfather who had served as a Russian fighter pilot in his youth.

Yulia and "Grandfather," as she affectionately called him, lived in an old, battered apartment building that was reminiscent of a bombed-out World War II structure. The frigid winter months with temperatures as low as forty below zero were challenging, and when Yulia reached the age of ten, Grandfather was no longer able to care for her. With nowhere else left to go, she was put in an orphanage in Kansk with eighty other children. The orphanage was called "Nadegda," which means "hope."

Yura was three years younger than Yulia and lived in a small village outside of Kansk. He was born out of wedlock as well. Yura and Yulia had the same birth mother, but different fathers. For a short time, Yura lived with his mother and father in a small home that could better be described as a shack. The father tried to make a living as a hunter, but, like the mother, drank too much vodka. Eventually, Yura's mother left his father and took the boy to live with her in Kansk. She often left Yura at home alone and she would disappear, sometimes for several days. During those times, Yura would feed and take care of himself, as well his baby sister, Luba. Yura's fate would, in the end, be the same as Yulia's. He was placed in the orphanage where she was. But, fortunately, their stories didn't end there.

Yulia's name is now Hannah Grace and Yura's name is Grant. They are citizens of the United States. Their last name is Merrill, and I'm their dad. Theirs is a story with a new, happy beginning, one of hope and love. The reason? Through adoption, Hannah Grace and Grant were shown that they have immeasurable value in who they are. No matter where they came from, no matter how they lived or what they did, they are priceless children who now have parents who will love them and lead them in life. But that's not the case for most children in Russia, where 60 percent of the babies are born out of wedlock and into alcoholism. They come into this world without a father, and many times also without a mother, to care for them, to raise them, and to help them understand their value and worth.

Happy beginnings don't always take place in the United States either. On a Sunday night about ten years ago, my wife, Susan, and I went to a meeting at our church. As the meeting was ending, two girls strolled in from outside where it was dark. Nobody knew who they were. Susan started talking to them and found out that their names were Eileen and Amanda and that they were "just looking for a ride to a friend's house." After Susan waded through more of their circumstances, she learned that they had run away from a juvenile detention facility the day before, and they both had heartbreaking stories. One of them said she had been raped by her father, and her mother was dead. The other girl not only didn't have a father, but was beaten by her mother. Her arms were scarred from "cutting," a form of self-mutilation. Soon after leaving the juvenile facility, the girls had been picked up on the side of the road by two men who apparently raped them.

These two little girls were only thirteen years old. They were running away from something they didn't want. But they didn't know what they were running to. They were scared, they were confused, and they were angry. Many people might shake their heads and call them "just a couple of troubled teens." But are they really just "problem children"? Or is there more to it? Think about it. In both cases they had AWOL (Absent Without Leave) dads. One father was physically absent. He had checked out. The other was emotionally absent and sexually abusive.

Sadly, Eileen and Amanda aren't the exception. There are countless children in our country on the run, trying to escape something. They have no idea who they are, where they belong, or what they value. They're scared, they're confused, and they're angry. These are powerful emotions for a child to handle. It's understandable that children are angry. Consider this:

- Thirty-four percent of children in the United States live without their father.[1]
- Sixty-two percent of children in prison grew up without a dad.[2]

And there are many more homes where the father is physically present but emotionally absent.

- Americans, fathers included, spend an average of four hours a day watching television.[3]
- On average, married fathers spend less than one hour a day interacting with their children.[4]

Indeed, fathers who are in their homes are working harder and putting in longer hours so they can do more for their children. They want to give them laptops, Xboxes, cell phones, designer clothes, and new cars. Why? Are they giving them gadgets to keep them preoccupied and more stuff to help them fit in? Are they trying to help them find their value according to our culture's standards? They may be giving their kids what they think they want, but it's not what they need.

IMAGE VERSUS IDENTITY

What our children, and all of us, really need is to know our makeup—how we are put together—because self-awareness in this area is key to loving and leading in relationships. And the first step to knowing our makeup is to understand our true identity because our value lies in our identity—who we are. We often hear people talk about their identity and image, but they are not the same thing. And understanding the difference between our identity versus our image is central to knowing ourselves.

Your Image

Let's start with image. Most of us are not quite sure how to answer the question, "Who am I?" So we end up trying to define who we are by putting ourselves together based on how we want others to see us. This can be especially true of teens and young adults.

Just what is our image? Our image is how we think others view us. If you look around in any direction, you'll see people who are spending a lot of energy, time, and money creating and re-creating an image they want to convey to others. It's a lot of work to keep up with what we think others want to see. Body piercings, tattoos, hairstyles, and social networking, as well as shoes, clothes, cars, and homes, are often used to convey that image.

Why are we so focused on image? First, because more often than not we're mostly concerned about ourselves and with what others think about us. We are this way because, deep down, we don't know who we really are. Second, some of us have been conditioned to think that we're valuable only if others think we're valuable. Let me explain. Elephants have great memories but aren't very smart. When they are babies, trainers stake them down. They will try to tug away from the stake thousands of times before they realize that they can't get loose. When they are older and much larger, these enormous animals can easily pull the stake out, but their "elephant memory" takes over, and they think for the rest of their lives that they can never get away from this stake.

When you were younger, did you hear voices that hammered away at you, that caused you to question your worth? Maybe someone said to you, "You aren't smart enough." Possibly someone else whispered in your ear, "You're not big enough." Still another shouted, "Can't you do anything right?" They drove a mental stake into your mind that kept you from understanding your immense value, a stake that held you back from being who God created you to be and from doing what He designed you to do. Many of us have never been able to tug away from those mental stakes that have been driven into our minds and hearts, and we continually yearn to find the "real me." In the process, we manufacture false images of ourselves to fill the void.

In our attempt to manufacture those false images, we often follow the crowd. But that may take us to a place where we don't want to end up. Consider this story. On July 8, 2005, the villagers of Gevas, Turkey, reportedly witnessed a sheep, which had wandered away, walk off a nearby cliff. But, the story doesn't end there. Suddenly, all the other sheep decided to follow. Fifteen hundred sheep worth over $100,000 walked off that cliff to the rocks below.[5] They didn't know they were going to a very bad place, only that they were following the sheep in front of them. That's what can happen to us, and our children, when image is all consuming. We just follow the crowd, sometimes in ways that can cause us great pain.

Remember trying to be cool, to fit in? It's the same today. Teens still want to be part of the crowd, and they still feel the pressure to do what everyone else is doing. In the movie *What a Girl Wants*, teenage Daphne is trying to be someone she's not and is really struggling with it. At one point, her boyfriend asks, "Why are you trying so hard to fit in, when you were born to stand out?"[6] Let's encourage our children to be different, to have the courage to do what's right and the conviction to stand out in the crowd.

I'm not saying that image is something we should ignore. It's important that others, especially our children, view us as men of good character and good models to follow. I'm just suggesting that our true value does not lie in our image.

Your Identity

As Tony Dungy and I discussed this important issue of image versus identity, he cut right to the chase. "Many times, we focus so much on our image because we think that image can carry the day, but it will only get you so far. Your identity, who you really are, is what makes you effective as a leader, not your image."[7] Knowing your identity is all-important. You can only give others what you've got. And it is only when you understand your own identity that you can effectively lead your children to understand theirs.

So let's turn our attention to identity. If someone at a get-together said to you, "Tell me about yourself," how would you respond? Maybe something like, "Well, I'm a business manager. I live in north Atlanta. I like to play tennis. I like to fish. I'm married, have two kids and a dog." You may give a "census bureau" answer—your vocation, hobbies, marital status, and number of kids. And that would be a good answer to the question because the person wanted to know *about* you. But that's not your identity. Your identity is not determined by what you do for a living, where you live, how much you have in your bank account, the car you drive, or the house you buy.

But if I were to go a bit deeper and ask you, "Who *are* you?" how would you answer? With a quizzical look on your face, you may say, "What do you mean?" Or, you may say something like, "Hmmm . . . Well, I'm Jonathan Taylor, the son of John and Sally Taylor. I'm a husband to Karen. I'm a father to one boy and one girl. I have two brothers and one sister." Those things are certainly part of your identity and are valuable. But what if you didn't have a father in your life when you were growing up? What if you were placed in foster care as a child and were raised by others? What if you're divorced? Do any of those things make you any less valuable? Of course not. Your ultimate identity is what gives you your ultimate value. So what is your identity and how do you discover it?

In 2007, a Swiss art collector paid $19,000 for what was presumed to be a nineteenth-century German portrait. Then, in 2009, it was discovered that the portrait was actually painted by Leonardo da Vinci and worth more than $150,000,000.[8] The painting's value was always there, but it wasn't known for centuries. In the same way, your value has been there since the beginning of time; maybe you just didn't know it. And your value rests on the canvas of your identity.

Your identity is one, and one thing only—who you are as a person. You were created exclusively by God and for God. This is your true identity. And God does not create junk. There were no flaws in your design and no errors in your construction. Additionally, there is no one else in the entire world like you. You are absolutely unique. You have unique DNA. Your one-of-a-kind status is also displayed in your fingerprints. Did you know that you even boast unique "eye prints"? The human iris, the colored part of our eye, is absolutely unique, even between twins.

Dr. Ben Carson, renowned pediatric neurosurgeon at Johns Hopkins University, has lived an amazing life, especially considering the poverty he lived in and the broken home he came from. He made medical history by being the first surgeon in the world to successfully separate Siamese twins conjoined at the back of the head. Dr. Carson's life story was made into a movie, *Gifted Hands*, which I enjoyed watching a few months after I had met him over lunch.

Dr. Carson mentioned to me that he was doing an interview a few years ago when the interviewer said, "Dr. Carson, I notice that you don't talk about race very much. Why is that?" Dr. Carson replied, "It's because I'm a neurosurgeon. When I go to the operating room and I peel back the scalp and I take off that bone flap and I open the dura, I am then operating on the thing that makes that person who they are. The covering doesn't make them who they are. It is the actual brain that does. And even though it may look the same in all people, obviously, it creates different people." Dr. Carson went on to say that each person's brain is "unique in function and makes them who they are. It is their imprint."9

So it's true. After God made you, He threw away the mold. You are a one-of-a-kind masterpiece. You are hand-made, custom-designed, and fully loaded by God. Why did God go to all that trouble to make a specially crafted you? Because He has a reason for you—a designed purpose—as a man and father, which we'll talk about more in the chapter on mind-set. So you've already got the basic framework, your identity, to be a loving and leading All Pro Dad. We just need to build upon that framework. Let's keep building as we explore your gifts.

Image	vs.	Identity
How others view you		Who you really are
Manufactured		Conceived
Changes		Never changes
Short-term value		Eternal value
Responds to external influences		Relies on internal qualities
Relative value		Immeasurable value
Common and shared		Unique

YOUR GIFTS

As part of our makeup, we also possess certain gifts, some-times called strengths. In this sense, a gift is simply an inherent, distinguishing attribute, quality, or characteristic. It can be physical, mental, or emotional. Unlike our identities, these qualities, which are ingrained in us by both nature and nurture, are not unique to just us. But each of us does have gifts or strengths that set us apart. You've probably had these gifts most, or all, of your life. You just didn't know it, and you may not know how to tap into them. Remember Dorothy in *The Wizard of Oz*? She always had the power in her red shoes to go home. She just needed to know it and then learn how to use that power.

Let me ask you a question. Has anyone ever communicated your gifts and potential so clearly to you that it profoundly influenced your life and helped define who you are today? Think back. Maybe it was your fourth-grade teacher, maybe your high school coach, maybe your best friend, maybe your mom or dad. Someone saw your potential, your unique gifts. They may have told you, "You have a beautiful voice," and now you're a singer. They told you, "You're good with kids," and now you're a teacher. "You have an awesome mechanical mind," someone said, and you became an engineer. You heard from someone, "You're really good with numbers," and now you're an accountant. Or another said to you, "You really care about people when they are sick," and now you're a nurse or doctor. Their loving words of affirmation inspired you to become what you are today.

As I sat in Truett Cathy's spacious but modest office, the ninety-year-old founder and CEO of Chick-fil-A and one of Forbes 400 Richest Americans shared with me how he lived through a depression and several wars. He also lived through the dark days of not having a loving father involved in his life.

While his father was in the home, Truett didn't have much of a relationship with him and certainly never got any loving words of validation or support from him. "I had a paper route," Truett shared. "But my father would never get up on Sunday mornings and help me with my paper route, even if it was raining or icy. Even if I had a fever, he would never, never get up and help me. He didn't want to be disturbed. I knew we better not disturb him."

Truett then sat up and said proudly, "There was a man that had a great influence on my life, Theo Abby, my Sunday school teacher. When I needed him, he would get up early in the morning to help me with my paper route. It was dark most of the time, so he would spot my papers." Theo Abby loved Truett and taught him the importance of faith, family, and a good work ethic. He also pointed out Truett's areas of giftedness. Years later, Truett started teaching Sunday school to teenage boys. He did so for over half a century, and, of course, founded the incredibly successful Chick-fil-A restaurants. Theo validated Truett with his words and actions. As a result, he had a huge impact on Truett's life.[10]

Perhaps you never had a dad, mom, teacher, coach, or friend who communicated to you the great strengths and potential they saw in you. If that's the case, here's one easy way to find out what your gifts are. Just ask five family members or friends, "In one or two words, what do you think is my single greatest strength?" While there might be one or two stray answers, the majority will probably give you the same response. And when they tell you, it will not be a surprise. They are just confirming something that you've probably known all along. You just needed someone to bring it to light and affirm it to you.

Many years ago, Bobb Biehl of Masterplanning Group International introduced me to this idea of identifying my greatest strength. He also challenged me, as he has done for countless others, to determine what it was. When I asked five friends and family members, I received several very similar answers. However, I boiled their responses down to one word: *catalyst.* A catalyst is an agent that provokes change or gets things going. At the same time, I also realized that one of my weaknesses was implicit in that strength. I am not particularly skilled at managing people or things over the long haul. So, if you want to launch a new product, program, or event, I might be able to put together the strategy and field the team to do so. Just don't let me manage it!

VALIDATING YOUR CHILD'S IDENTITY

Validating a child's identity is essential. Without some sort of validation, many children grow up spending a lifetime searching for their identity. Children burn a lot of energy always trying to prove themselves worthy to their mom or dad. And once children are grown, if they leave the home without feeling validated, they will start searching the world to find acceptance. They will become adults who forever seek attention, affirmation, and acceptance—in all of the wrong places. They will strive to prove their manhood or womanhood to both themselves and others through their sexual encounters, economic success, and other countless dead-end ways.

As Plato said, it's important to "know thyself." Not so you can become egocentric or self-serving, but so that you will know, in turn, how to help your children know themselves and understand their wonderful worth.

All of our children need to hear incredible words of affirmation from us. They need to first clearly understand their value. We must love and lead our children by validating them for who they are—masterpieces, unique creations with immeasurable value. They are priceless! How do we do so? We can tell them, as I've always done with my children, that I love them "no matter what." Our children need to know that we love them for who they are, not for what they do or don't do. We can dislike or be disappointed in something they say or do, but nothing should ever separate them from our love.

For some time after our son Grant came from Russia at the age of nine to be part of our family, he purposefully defied Susan and me, lashing out in anger. He was intentionally trying to push us away. Becoming attached to us only to be abandoned again was a very real and scary thought for him. There were many occasions when I looked him in the eyes and said, "Grant, Mom and I love you no matter what you do or say. We will never leave you or forsake you!" Validate your child's value.

VALIDATING YOUR CHILD'S GIFTS

Parents, teachers, and coaches say it. I'm sure Susan and I have said it a few times to our kids: "You can be anything you want to be." But it's a lie. In all fairness to us parents, our intention is not to lie. We say it because we want to encourage them; we want to pump them up. We want them to dream big. The problem is that when we tell them they can do anything, we may be setting them up for future discouragement. I wonder how many of the kids who audition for *American Idol* were told by someone they could sing well when, in reality, they couldn't hold a tune if their lives depended on it. The truth is, none of us can be anything or do anything we want. I can tell you, without a doubt in my mind, that I never could have played in the NBA. It's not in my genes.

But our children all have areas that they are truly gifted in. So why not affirm our children in these areas? As our children were growing up, Susan and I recognized and verbally validated each of our children in their gifts. We noticed that our oldest daughter Megan had the uncanny ability to read and size up people very quickly. She is very good in relationships. Emily is our creative one. Acting, singing, painting, and creative writing are all in her sweet spot. Hannah has an analytical mind and loves to debate. Marky has always been the kind of guy everyone wants to be with. His hand-eye coordination has helped him in sports as well. Grant has an engineering mind. He can fix just about anything.

Actress Judy Garland once said, "Always be a first-rate version of yourself, instead of a second-rate version of somebody else."[11] We need to encourage our children to be themselves and to focus on their God-given gifts.

More Ways to Validate Your Child's Identity and Gifts

We can affirm our kids by cheering them on. We can also affirm our child's identity and gifts in a letter. Our Family First program for fathers, All Pro Dad, holds events with NFL teams at their stadiums across the country. One thing we do at these major gatherings of fathers and their children is to have the men write a short letter to their child. Although they are free to write anything they desire, we encourage them to include at least the following three things in their notes:

- First, tell your child that you love them for who they are. For example, in a letter to one of my kids, I wrote, "I love you for just being you. You are an incredible young woman, a child of God created with immeasurable value and worth. I love you always, no matter what." My words conveyed my unconditional love to my daughter.
- Second, describe and praise your son or daughter for his or her unique talents, gifts, and abilities. I wrote to my child, "For many years I have noticed that you are a leader. Your friends like to follow you in what you do. You have a magnetic personality and other people like to be around you."
- Third, tell them what you want them to remember about your relationship. In my letter I wrote, "I want

you to always remember that spending time with you is a #1 priority for me. Just being with you is something I always cherish."

This simple gesture from a father to his son or daughter has proven to have a major impact in many of their relationships. This doesn't have to be done in a football stadium. You can write the letter at your kitchen table.

Before we go on, there is something else you can begin to think about doing as a loving leader in your home. There is a simple, yet profound, ceremony that you, as a father, can hold that will validate your child. It's sometimes called a "rite of passage" or "blessing."

There are rites of passage and ceremonies in many cultures that memorialize the birth of a child, puberty, graduation, engagement, marriage, death, and other stages of life. In our Western culture, while we still celebrate marriage through a wedding ceremony and observe death through a funeral, we lack, with the notable exception of the Bar Mitzvah and Bat Mitzvah in the Jewish faith, a generally accepted rite of passage from childhood into adulthood that occurs around the time of puberty.

What is a blessing? The Hebrew word for "to bless" is *baruch*. It means literally "a good word." When we bless our child, we are placing our "seal of approval" upon them and giving them power to prosper in many areas of life, including marriage, parenthood, finances, health, and career.

Why do children need the blessing of their parents? A ceremonial blessing is an act of the parents recognizing the passage of a son or daughter emotionally and spiritually into manhood or womanhood. It helps to establish his or her identity, gifts, and purpose as an adult. When we release our children into this new season in life, we are releasing them to take on more responsibility and decision making. It also must be said that there is something inside every child that makes that child crave a good word of blessing or "seal of approval" from his or her parents. Our boys need to know that "they've got what it takes." Our girls need to know they are beautiful inside and out.

I've had such a ceremony for three of our children so far. You can get ideas for how to put something together and what to say during the occasion on my blog, MarkMerrill.com.

Validating Your Spouse's Identity and Gifts

As All Pro Dads, we also need to speak the same life-giving encouragement of identity and gifts to our wives. Winston Churchill, the great British prime minister, had the right idea. Toward the end of his life, Churchill was at a dinner party where someone asked him this question: "If you could not be who you are, who would you like to be?" Churchill thought for a second, stood up, turned to his wife, and said, "Mrs. Churchill's second husband."[12] At that very moment, her heart must have melted. In essence, he was saying that his wife was so valuable that there is no one he'd rather be than her husband. Talk about validation! Make it a point to encourage your wife in this way this week.

The Benefits of Validating Your Home Team

Validation of each family member's identity and gifts benefits not only the individual but also your entire home team. Think of it this way: Each player on a sports team has a designated, critical role to fill. On a football team, a quarterback has the center, offensive guards, and offensive tackles to protect him; wide receivers to pass the ball to; running backs to hand off to; as well as tight ends and fullbacks. They all have a purpose, and when the plays are executed well, they often score points. In the same way, our spouse, children, parents, and grandparents all have different but equally significant roles in the functioning of the family. Working together, the whole team is lifted up.

Realizing that we, and our children, are special, that we have something to offer, will confirm in our hearts and minds that we can have a positive impact on others in this world. To live otherwise can be heartrending. Former governor Jeb Bush recently shared with me, "I've always thought my dad [former United States president George H. W. Bush] was near perfect and still do. But in my early twenties, I realized I didn't have to be just like him. I could be my own person and could create my own path, and I could still love my dad."[13] Jeb got it right. He knew that he had a unique identity and special gifts. He wasn't like anyone else and didn't have to try to be like anyone else, including his father.

When we know our makeup, our capacity to love will grow. As we confirm our own unique identity and gifts, we can love and serve our spouse and children by affirming their value and strengths as well. And from that love for our family, we will earn the right to lead them in all areas of life.

HUDDLE UP AND ASK YOUR CHILD:

1 What is most important—who you are or what people think of you? Why?

2 What are three words that describe you?

3 What is one thing you think you are really good at?

4 I've noticed you're really good at _____.

3

KNOW YOUR MIND-SET

What's My Purpose?

For as he thinks in his heart, so is he.

—Proverbs 23:7

They call it the "Bogeyman." It's a mind-set that many professional golfers have that causes them to putt more accurately from all distances when putting for par than when putting for birdie. Why? Because the players fear the bogey more than they desire the birdie. In a 2009 Wharton School, University of Pennsylvania study, the researchers who came to these conclusions estimated that this determination for avoiding a negative, a bogey, more than gaining an equal positive, a birdie—known in economics as loss aversion—costs the average pro golfer about one stroke per 72-hole tournament, and the top twenty golfers about $1.2 million in prize money a year.[1]

How golfers think, their mind-set, affects how they play. It's no different with dads. Many fathers, due to influences we'll explore, just focus on making par as a parent, rather than going for the win. A fear-of-failure mind-set often causes fathers and kids to lose precious opportunities for greatness in their relationships.

Mind-set is simply your way of thinking, your mental attitude, or your state of mind about something. Your mind-set as a man and a father is greatly influenced by your past. You are, to a certain extent, a product of your past. By past, I mean the time from your conception until the last word you just read on this page. Your upbringing, family, friends, books, our culture, and the media are just a few of the things that shape your current mind-set. Aside from your genetic disposition, two of the greatest past influences on your mind-set as a father are your father and the culture. So let's take a brief look at those influences that sometimes drive us to mediocrity in our thinking as fathers and then focus the rest of our time in this chapter on a new course of thinking that may just give you the winning edge you've been searching for with your kids.

Internal Influences—Your Father

While we don't want to dwell on it, it's important to understand that your father, good or bad or in between, greatly influenced your life. Your answers to questions like these impact how you think about fathering: Did you grow up with your father involved in your life? Was he physically present? Was he emotionally present? Did he spend much time with you? What were his beliefs? Were he and your mother married? How did he treat your mom? Did he drink too much or abuse drugs? Did he discipline you? Did he do it in anger? Did he affirm you?

Most men are not neutral about their fathers. If they had a loving example in their dad growing up, they are more likely to want to be and parent just like him. If their father was not there at all, or emotionally absent, some guys, unfortunately, will just follow in his footsteps. Others will want to be the exact opposite, sometimes out of bitterness, anger, or even hatred. But a man should want to be an All Pro Dad not to spite his father, but out of a compelling desire to love and lead his children.

EXTERNAL INFLUENCES—THE CULTURE

Former NFL player Joe Ehrmann, in the book *Season of Life*, says you and I have been influenced and taught by our culture that it takes three things to be a man: athletic ability, sexual conquest, and economic success. When those three things are checked off the list of life, then you are supposedly dubbed a man. But you and I know that if those are the marks of a man, then we will be left with a sense of despair, emptiness, and unhappiness once we get there. Ehrmann says that definition our culture teaches us is false masculinity.

Real masculinity, he says, is based on two things—relationships and having a cause beyond yourself. First, Ehrmann says masculinity "ought to be defined in terms of relationships" and "taught in terms of the capacity to love and to be loved."[2] Second, every man should have some kind of cause or purpose in life that's bigger than his own wants and desires. We'll talk more about this in our chapter about your Message.

There is also a lot of false thinking in our culture about the role of a father. The media definitely has shaped the way we think as fathers. Out of all the programs on TV right now, how many depict a strong man loving and leading his family? There are a few shining fatherhood lights from the past, like *The Cosby Show*, but for the most part, dads are portrayed in Homer Simpson–like buffoonery.

And this is not just limited to television. Musicians often sing about things like one-night stands with women they meet in bars, hoping their wives don't find out. Many sing or rap about men degrading women. And many Internet advertisers do their best to entice you away from being a "one woman" kind of man and to find "personal freedom" away from your family.

In addition to these media messages that downplay the importance of fatherhood and attempt to lure us from our most important job, we've been taught by our culture that a father is relegated to being a provider, protector, and punisher. And while it's true that a father should meet the financial needs of his family, protect them, and appropriately discipline his children, if that's all he does, he will have failed as a father.

Your Mind-set—A New Way of Thinking

I can't erase your way of thinking about fatherhood. And I don't want to. My guess is that you've learned many things over the years that have proven to be beneficial in your journey as a dad. Instead, I'd like to shift your thinking. I don't know your story and your mind-set, so I don't know what kind of shift you'll need to make. For you, it may mean a slight shift. Or it might be a 180-degree about-face in your thinking as a father—a brand-new way of thinking. While there may be some truth to us being products of our past, it does not mean that we are prisoners of our past. The old chains can be broken. But you have to know that there's not a single key to doing so. It will take a chisel and some time to break free from the old mind-set. Your past does not have to prescribe what you will be in the future.

So what's this new way of thinking? It's thinking of your role as a father as being your job—your most important job—because it is. That should be your mind-set.

You also have to understand your ultimate purpose and responsibilities in your job. What would you think of an executive if he didn't know the mission of his company? What about a football coach who didn't know the purpose for his team? What would be your reaction if a military general said he didn't understand his objectives on the battlefield? If a manager was never given a job description, do you think he'd understand the responsibilities of his position? You'd expect all of them to fail, and in some cases, maybe even be fired, right?

So if you agree that being a dad is your most important job and that you must know your purpose in that job, you need to be able to answer the following questions: What is my mission as a father? What are my goals and objectives as a dad? What daily or weekly tasks will I undertake to accomplish those goals? What is my job description as a father?

Are you going to be fired if you don't have all the answers? Of course not. But without an understanding of each of these things, you won't be the kind of dad you'd like to be to your children.

Before we address all of these items you need for your job, I'd like to make clear what your job is not. Your job is not that of a general contractor. A general contractor oversees a bunch of subcontractors who usually have skills in specific trades.

Some parents think that it's the schoolteacher's job to teach their kids everything. While it's true that a teacher instructs our children in certain subjects, his or her job does not include teaching our children manners. The Little League coach should help instruct a child in skills of throwing, catching, and hitting, but a father should support that instruction by playing catch in the backyard with his child. Hiring a running, throwing, or hitting coach can help, but it is not the only answer, especially for younger children. A youth pastor is to help the youth in a church with lessons and fellowship, not to be the lone source of your child's learning about faith and virtues of life. Your child's friends should be just that. Friends should not have to instruct your child about sex education, what movies to watch, and what music to listen to. You—not your neighbor, coach, friend, or youth pastor—have direct and ultimate authority over your child. Your job is that of a CEO in your home. You're the team leader.

Now that we have the mind-set that being a dad is our most important job, let's spend the rest of this chapter learning about our mission, goals, job description, and management responsibilities as a father.

Your Mission

When I think of the most mission-minded people I know of, I think of the Navy SEALs who have chosen that very lifestyle to protect their country. They are highly dedicated men who are in top physical and mental shape and are elite professionals in their field because they are sold out to their mission. The SEALs were created in 1962. The SEAL acronym stands for "Sea, Air, and Land," the elements in which they operate. No matter what the conditions, they will not be deterred.

To enlist as a Navy SEAL, one must first go through the rigorous and grueling SEAL training. Only 25 percent of those who enter into the thirty-month SEAL training become Navy SEALs. And one of the important lessons SEALs learn early on is the importance of mission and teamwork.[3]

But what makes these men an elite force? Howard Wasdin, former navy sniper and SEAL Team 6 member, says it is this: "Mental toughness. I can take just about anyone and make them physically strong. A lot of people showed up at [training] who were much more physically capable than I was, football players and athletes in phenomenal shape, and they were the first to quit. Mental toughness is a must to make it through training, much less through combat."[4]

SEAL Team 6 is made up of the top men in the SEAL program. These men from Virginia Beach, Virginia, seem like ordinary men on the surface, but they are heroes underneath. On May 1, 2011, in Abbottabad, Pakistan, SEAL Team 6 killed Osama bin Laden. Team 6 had a clear mission and began preparing for that mission well in advance in an exact replica of the two-story structure they were to invade. Leading up to the mission in Pakistan, Team 6 considered as many contingencies as possible.

On April 30, 2011, the team experienced a delay in the operation due to bad weather. While waiting, Team 6 reviewed the details of the plan once again. Team 6 would not be deterred from its mission. After the weather cleared, Team 6 boarded two helicopters and traveled to Abbottabad. The journey was clear, but upon landing, one of the Black Hawk helicopters clipped the compound wall, causing it to crash inside the compound. Thus the team was required to alter its plan to get to bin Laden. The SEALs from the second Black Hawk got onto the building by "fast-roping" from the chopper. Upon entering the compound, Team 6 encountered an armed Abu Ahmed al-Kuwaiti. He, his wife, his brother, and bin Laden's son were taken down during the mission. Osama bin Laden was found on the top floor in his room with his youngest wife. He gave no indication of surrender. As a result, he was shot with two rounds and killed. After only thirty-eight minutes, the mission was accomplished.[5]

Only a small group of military advisors and officials knew about this covert mission. And no one outside of SEAL Team 6, not even the president of the United States, knows who pulled the trigger. We just know that the mission was accomplished.

For a Navy SEAL, the mission is all-important. Other branches of the U.S. military boast the same thing. The United States Department of the Army Leadership Handbook outlines the Soldier's Creed, which in part states: "I will always place the mission first."

For a father, the mission is all-important and should always come first. Like a SEAL, the key to accomplishing that mission is mental toughness. It's a toughness that says, "No matter who is firing at me, even if it's friendly fire from my wife or children, I will not be deterred. I will take a bullet and even die for my family. My mission is all-important." And like a SEAL, much of the fatherhood mission is stealth.

No one will know the blood, sweat, and tears that you've poured into your mission, sometimes not even your wife. And there will be no parades for your heroic efforts and no Purple

Hearts awarded to you. But when all is said and done, you'll have the reward of knowing you gave it everything you've got and the reward of watching your children pass your love and leadership on to the next generation. And, hopefully, your greatest reward will be the words you hear from God in heaven: "Well done, thou good and faithful servant."

Pastor Tim Kizziar said, "Our greatest fear . . . should not be of failure but of succeeding at things in life that don't really matter."[6] A father's mission matters. So, what is our fatherhood mission? It's clear and straightforward: love and lead our family.

Your Goals

At Family First, when I'm working on developing our strategic plan with our team, I do my best to ensure that all of the goals stated in the plan will move us toward accomplishing the mission. The goals we establish as fathers should also help us achieve our mission of loving and leading our families.

In their best-selling book *The Love Dare*, authors Stephen and Alex Kendrick state that love is built on two pillars, patience and kindness. They suggest that other characteristics of love are extensions of these two attributes. Being patient and kind fathers are goals that many of us struggle with, but they are goals we need to reach for that will help us further our mission. Let's start with something I really struggle with—patience.

We live in a world of instant gratification. We want it all, and we want it now. We're a nation of express lanes, fast food, high-speed Internet, and smartphones. Sure, there are benefits, but it's a problem when we impose those same expectations on people. We demand instant acceptance from our peers, instant response from our employees, and instant help from our spouse, regardless of the circumstances. And when we don't get the immediate response we expect, we react negatively.

My kids have taught me a lot of things, and I can tell you, it's a very humbling experience. One thing that they've shown me over and over again is my lack of patience. For example, they've pointed out my impatience with the grocery store cashier during checkout, with the waitress at a restaurant, and while hurriedly driving them to school. You get the picture. It's kind of embarrassing to admit, but I was even impatient while in traffic today when my son Marky was with me. When my children point out my impatience or other faults, I can respond by being defensive and telling them to be quiet. Or, I can listen and thank them for pointing it out to me and ask them to keep reminding me. I'm pleased to report, I've been patiently doing the latter.

My wife also knows my struggle with patience. It was October 11, 2010. Susan was sitting across the table from me in the conference room at a Family First leadership team meeting. I received a text from Susan during the meeting at 10:47 a.m. I know the exact time because I saved the text as a constant reminder. It simply said, "Patience, kindness." She saw how I was being short and cutting people off in the meeting and gave me a gentle nudge in the right direction.

As I interviewed the business, sports, and other leaders I've quoted in this book, I determined that I'm not alone in my challenge to be patient. When I asked each of them, "What is your greatest weakness?" the vast majority answered, "Impatience." Norm Miller, founder and chairman of Interstate Batteries, may have provided at least one reason for this lack of patience: "It's hard when you are a driven person to be patient when someone is not thinking along the same line as you are or the same speed you are."[7]

Tony Dungy and I were on a deep-sea fishing trip and brought several other friends with us. We had been fishing for quite some time in the same hole and hadn't caught anything. Several of us type-A personalities started to get antsy and suggested we pull up anchor and find another spot to catch fish. Tony calmly said only three words: "Patience, men, patience." Well, shortly after that, we started hauling in some big grouper. Patience often reaps rewards. In this case, it certainly did.

Patience is a choice. When you're patient, you choose to hold your tongue instead of releasing its venom. You choose to have a long fuse instead of a quick temper. Patience is choosing to control your emotions rather than letting your emotions control you.

Patience has to do with your *attitude* toward others.

Kindness, the other pillar of love, has to do with your *actions* toward others. Authors Stephen and Alex Kendrick further say, "Kindness is love in action. If patience is how love reacts in order to minimize a negative circumstance, kindness is how love acts to maximize a positive circumstance. Patience avoids a problem; kindness creates a blessing. One is preventive, the other proactive."[8]

Author Leo Buscaglia once wrote about a contest he was asked to judge. The purpose of the contest was to identify the most caring child. The winner was a four-year-old boy whose next-door neighbor was an elderly man who had recently lost his wife. One day, the little boy saw the man crying. So, he walked into the old gentleman's yard, climbed onto his lap, and just sat there. When his mother asked him what he said to the man, the little boy said, "Nothing, I just helped him cry."[9]

That little boy showed kindness to the old man. And kindness is one of the great pillars of love. Author Rick Warren says there are four things we need to do to show kindness to others:

1. *See needs of people all around us*—physical, emotional, and spiritual needs. That means you and I need to stop and look. Be observant. The little boy saw the need.
2. *Sympathize with people's pain and struggles.* We've got to identify and empathize with them, feel what they feel. The little boy sympathized with the old man.

3. *Seize the moment.* Do what we can, when we can. Don't wait. It's okay that you're interrupted. It's okay that it's inconvenient. The little boy promptly went to help the old man. He seized the moment.

4. *Spend lavishly to meet the need.* We should give our time, talent, and treasure to others without expecting anything in return. The little boy spent time just sitting there in the old man's lap and helping him cry.[10]

The little boy loved that man. He saw, he sympathized, he seized, he spent.

It was halftime at the Plant High School junior varsity football game. Plant was leading by a wide margin. My son had been playing strong safety the entire first half. I was fired up about seeing him come out the second half and, hopefully, make some big plays. As the whistle blew and the ball was kicked off to start the remainder of the game, I couldn't find my son. "Where is he?" I asked my wife. She shrugged her shoulders. Then we looked down on the sidelines and spotted him out of his uniform.

After the game our son, a man of few words, did not give much of an explanation. But another parent had heard what happened. There weren't enough uniforms for all the boys, so Marky had given up his uniform to another boy who hadn't played all season so that he could play. Admittedly, my son probably realized he wouldn't have played much, if at all, in the second half because of the lopsided score, so that made doing what he did a bit easier. Nevertheless, Susan and I were so grateful for what he did. He saw, sympathized, seized, and spent.

An Iowa truck driver named Mark Lemke wrote to *Sports Illustrated* several years ago. He nominated his nineteen-year-old son, Cory, for an award the magazine gives to exceptional athletes. Lemke said Cory had set all kinds of golf records and he wanted to honor his son who had just died the week before in a tragic motorcycle accident. *Sports Illustrated* then wrote about Lemke's story.

Hundreds of miles away in Indianapolis, Indiana, Tony Dungy, then head coach of the Indianapolis Colts, read the article, was moved by it, and called Lemke to encourage him and see how he could help. You see, Dungy had lost his son James about six months earlier. After the call, Dungy continued to keep in touch with Lemke, brought him as his guest to the Super Bowl, and even spent time visiting with him the day before the big game. Tony Dungy saw the need, sympathized with him, seized the moment, and spent his time to shower kindness upon Mark Lemke. And that's just one stranger whom Tony Dungy has helped. I know of many others. This extremely busy man gives of himself, all with no pay and no expectation of reward or anything else in return. He loved that man with his kindness.

Kindness is contagious. You may have seen the Liberty Mutual television commercials that show how one act of kindness begets another act of kindness, which then begets another and another. One of the spots shows a man picking up a doll for a little girl in a stroller. Later, the mother of the little girl is in a coffee shop and sees a man's coffee on the edge of the table. She pushes it in so it doesn't spill. Another man sees her act and helps a guy who falls on the sidewalk in the rain, and so on.

If it's true, as Stephen and Alex Kendrick suggest, that love is built on patience and kindness, then the foundation upon which those pillars stand is selflessness. As we've seen in this chapter, patience and kindness can only stand if we are serving and giving to others, looking not just to our own interests but also to the interests of other people. Those pillars collapse when we're only thinking about what we've got to say, what we've got to do, and where we've got to be.

Your Job Description—CEO of the Family

As you pursue this new mind-set as a father—that being a dad is your most important job—you'll want to have a job description that outlines your duties as you serve in the distinguished role as CEO of your family. Just remember, your job description doesn't cover everything you do; it simply provides an overview of your responsibilities.

Here are ten essentials of your position.

1. Love Your Wife

Actively loving your wife will radically strengthen your marriage and will also be incredibly beneficial to your children. The number one source of security for kids is when they know that their dad loves their mother and is steadfastly committed to her for life. If you are not married to your child's mother, you can still exhibit patience and kindness in your relationship with her no matter what she says or does.

2. Spend Time with Your Kids

How you spend your time is a reflection of what's important to you. If you value your kids, you'll want to be with them. Build monuments with and for your children that will create memories that will last a lifetime. We'll talk more about how you can build those memorable monuments in our chapter on knowing your Method.

3. Be a Role Model

It's impossible to underestimate the importance of a father modeling the type of behavior he desires to see in his children. Role models don't just talk the talk; they walk the walk of an honorable man. A great place to start is consistency. We'll talk more about this in our chapter on being a role model. Want to be your children's hero? Then be what you want your children to be.

4. Understand and Enjoy Your Children

Like you, every child has unique DNA, unique finger-prints, and a unique personality. We discussed that in the chapter on Makeup. In order to be the best father you can be, you'll need to understand your children as individuals. You'll also want to know what each of your children needs from you the most. One may need encouragement. Another may respond better with affection. Remember, too, how quickly your kids grow up, and just enjoy being with them.

5. Show Affection

Children long for a secure place in this fast-paced world. They find it most often in the warm embrace of a parent. As children grow, so does their need for acceptance and a sense of belonging. Such a need is met when a father offers a hug, or a kind word, and expresses his appreciation and love for his children. But showing affection doesn't stop there. Make sure to say, "I love you" every day.

6. Secure Your Family's Financial Future

Financial stress is one of the leading factors that tears families apart. In order to put your family in a position of strength, you have to shore up your finances. First, hate debt. Do everything you can to get out of it as quickly as possible. Then, make sure you establish a budget that not only trims expenses but also allows you to save and share with those in need. Have proper insurance. Finally, make sure you live and teach these frugal principles to your children as well.

7. Eat Together as a Family

Most children today don't know the meaning of a family dinnertime. Yet the communication and unity built during this time is integral to a healthy family life. Sharing a meal together—breakfast, lunch, or dinner—provides structure to an often hectic schedule. It also gives kids the opportunity to talk about their lives. This is a time for fathers to listen as well as give advice and encouragement.

8. Discipline with a Gentle Spirit

True discipline is a function of a father's love for his children, which is why it should never be hard-nosed or harsh. The role of discipline is not to intimidate or tear down but to mold and correct. Correcting your kids should be done in private, and you and your wife should be unified in how you discipline. Strive to be consistent.

9. Pray and Worship Together

Families that have a healthy prayer life and take worshipping God seriously help their children understand that there is an ultimate authority in their lives—an authority who provides moral absolutes for them to live by. Every child needs to know that there is right and wrong, good and evil. Living under the authority of God will give them that knowledge.

10. Realize You're a Father Forever

Someday every father must let go. As he allows his children their freedom to direct their own lives, a good father realizes that he doesn't abandon them at a dorm room, a wedding altar, or the door of their first job. He continues to encourage, coach, and convey his wisdom to his children forever.

4 Cs FOR THE CEO

Most CEOs have certain management responsibilities. As CEO of your family, part of your responsibility is to manage your children well. A father has to have a manager mind-set. Let me illustrate. How do you handle management at the office? You probably meet regularly with those who report directly to you and spend time training them. Your goal is to train them so well that they'll be able to take your job one day and hopefully do an even better job than you did. That's what we should want as fathers too.

Here are four Cs to help you in your management responsibilities of your children.

Communication

"Communication has been the number one thing in our family," Grammy Award–winning Michael W. Smith said to me with great confidence. "Just being able to always communicate what you're feeling is so important. I think a lot of times families get in trouble when they stop communicating. Somebody gets his or her feelings hurt and then somebody gets defensive and then you just stop talking. You start doing that for long periods of time and the gap gets wider and it's just always harder to recover. It's always about communicating and keeping the lines of communication open with Deb and me in our marriage, and with our kids."

Part of managing your home is communicating well with those you have authority over. Connecting with younger children is a bit easier. Staying connected with your teens is more challenging. Here are four things you can do to effectively keep the lines of communication open with your teen.

1. **Be calm.** When you approach a teen while filled with a lot of emotion, such as anger, anxiety, or enthusiasm, the teen may feel pressured to comply. That approach doesn't work because teens crave independence. They see themselves as older and capable, and as a result they want to make more decisions for themselves. Instead, try approaching your teen calmly and be open to discussion. This will take the pressure off the teen and keep the conversation from escalating into opposition.

2. **Be confident.** Teens can be very persuasive, and as their persuasive ability increases, you may lose your confidence and begin to doubt yourself. If your teen is persuasive and persistent, the confidence goes even

more quickly as the teen wears you out. Stand firm and know when you are weakening. Enlist your spouse to pinch-hit for you and interface with your teen for a while. Another option is to have a friend be a sounding board for your doubts and encourage you.

3. **Be clear.** Make your request clear and have the details of the request firmly in your mind, or better yet, written out on paper. All children know how best to win over, or distract, their parents. Teens are children with a lot of years of experience. Do not let them distract you with other issues; stick to the clear request you have outlined.

4. **Be concise.** Long, complicated speeches are exasperating to teens, especially after listening to seven teachers for seven hours every school day. Present your request calmly, confidently, clearly, and concisely. Do not make it a big deal. Listen to your teen's response, acknowledge what they say, and then either modify your request or restate it again. If they agree to your request, acknowledge it positively. If they do not agree, do not engage; simply tell them you will discuss it with them again in a few days. Then walk away and let them think about it.

Any good CEO and communicator also monitors those who report to him. The same applies to our children. Here's a GPS device to help you keep track of your children. *G* stands for Geography. Know where your kids are going. *P* stands for

People. Know who they will be spending time with. *S* stands for Specifics. Know what they will be doing and exactly when they're expected to be home. Know your child's GPS at all times. Just the other night, my son asked, "Dad, can I go to John's house?" My response was typical. Since I already knew where he was going, I proceeded to ask, "Who else is going to be there?"

Marky responded, "Robert and Paul."

"And what are you going to do?" I asked further.

"Play Xbox."

"Okay, please be home by 11:30."

"Okay, Dad."

And then I closed with my signature phrase, "Have fun, honor God."

Perhaps you've heard it said, "People don't do what we expect, they do what we inspect." That applies to our children as well. Another part of monitoring and communicating with our kids is to inspect things. We need to inspect their homework and report card to ensure they're getting their job done. We need to monitor what they're doing on the Internet and smartphone as well.

Calendar

A typical day for parents can be hectic:

6:00 a.m.—get the kids up

6:15 a.m.—try again to get the kids up

6:30 a.m.—breakfast, get the kids dressed

7:00 a.m.—take the kids to school

7:05 a.m.—go back home to get the homework
        they forgot, back to school, off to work
3:00 p.m.—pick kids up from school

Then ballet, baseball, football, piano, and help with homework. Cook dinner, do homework again, then to bed.

So many of us have an "airlines approach" to scheduling. Airlines routinely overbook their flights and often end up having to bump some stressed-out passengers to different flights. We can become a little stressed ourselves when we leave no margin and overbook our children's schedules and our own schedules. An overly booked schedule can be the culprit that causes pressure in a family. Our busy schedules plus our children's busy schedules equals missed opportunities to enjoy life and one another. To release some of that pressure, an effective CEO says no to more things outside the home and yes to more things inside. When our children were younger, Susan and I found that youth sports were a good thing, but even too much of a good thing can be a bad thing. So our general rule was one sport at a time. Just remember, your family's calendar and activities reflect what's important to you.

And managing the family calendar is not just mom's responsibility. You have many important work appointments on your Outlook calendar, so why not include appointments for your kids? Parent/teacher conferences, sports, extracurricular activities, exams, doctor appointments, trips, work days in the yard, and nights out with your son or daughter should all be part of your calendar as a father. I'll talk more about this in the chapter on knowing your Method.

Chores

Are you tired of getting no response when you ask your kids to take out the garbage, do the dishes, or pick up their room? Well, as you manage your home well, you'll want to have a chore chart and be sure to assign age-appropriate chores to your children. When our kids were growing up, we made a chore chart. In the vertical column on the left, we listed all their chores, including things like taking out the garbage, washing the dishes, yard work, making their beds, and cleaning their rooms. On the horizontal row at the top, we wrote each of their names. As they completed a chore, they checked it off and then we reviewed it with them at the end of the week and awarded them with an allowance.

By doing chores, our children learn the value of hard work and its rewards. As they do chores, we also have opportunities to teach them important life lessons. I remember doing some weeding in our yard with my children when they were young. When I noticed them getting bored, I tossed out a question: "What would happen if we didn't weed?"

"Well," said my oldest daughter, "all the good stuff would die."

I went on to explain how that's true in our lives as well, and had them tell me some of the "weeds" we all need to watch for. They came up with things like calling people names, lying, and being mean to other children. We talked about how weeds choke out our joy and hurt our relationships.

I wrapped up this mini life lesson by sharing this truth: "Just like in the yard, if we don't get rid of the weeds in our lives, the weeds will get rid of the good stuff."

Checkbook

Financial issues are among the most prevalent reasons for marriage failure. According to a 2009 Utah State University study, one of the best indicators of marital discord is what it terms "financial disagreements." Couples who "reported disagreeing about finances once a week were over 30 percent more likely to divorce over time than couples who reported disagreeing about finances a few times per month."[11] People tend to be emotional and reactive, rather than strategic, when discussing finances. But it's imperative to have a plan to avoid pressure. Financial expert Dave Ramsey suggests three initial goals in your plan: establish a $1,000 emergency fund, eliminate debt, and have three to six months of savings set aside so that when the pressure starts to get too high, you have an avenue for release.[12]

As you start to get a better grip on your finances, show your children how to be good stewards of money as well. Teach your children how to save, spend, and share wisely. In our home, as our children were growing up, each of our children had three mason jars for the allowance or "commission" they earned for doing their chores. They received a fifty-cent increase each year on their birthday. So a ten-year-old would receive five dollars per week. Two dollars would be placed in the spend jar. Two dollars and fifty cents was deposited into the save jar, and fifty cents in the share jar, to be given to church.

Love your children well as the CEO of your family. Train your children well by focusing on the 4 Cs for the CEO—Communication, Calendar, Chores, and Checkbook.

As a father, you must have the mind-set that being a dad is your most important job. And like a Navy SEAL, your mission comes first. You must execute your fatherhood mission of loving and leading your children with unwavering resolve and sheer determination. Your goals, your job description, your responsibilities as CEO of your family should exist only to enable you to accomplish that ultimate mission as a dad.

HUDDLE UP AND ASK YOUR CHILD:

1   What is one thing you're really afraid of? Why?

2   On a scale of 1 to 10, how patient am I with you?

3   What is one thing I can do to be more patient?

4   On a scale of 1 to 10, how kind am I to our family?

5   Do you remember a time when I wasn't kind? When? How did I handle it?

4

KNOW YOUR MOTIVE

Why Do I Do What I Do?

Everyone thinks of changing the world,
but no one thinks of changing himself.

—Leo Tolstoy

Thursday, October 14, 2010. It was an emotionally painful morning. I had been frustrated for a few days about a number of different things that weren't going as I expected. In retrospect, some of the things were so insignificant that I don't even remember what they were.

Over the years, I've found that when circumstances and things affect me adversely, the person closest to me, Susan, is the one I shoot my frustration at. Well, on this particular morning, I asked Susan to meet me at a restaurant for coffee to talk. Susan and I have found that meeting in a public place is a good way to ensure that emotions are kept in check, especially when we're talking about a tough topic.

My real motive in calling the meeting was to talk to her about how I thought she wasn't making our marriage a priority recently. It seemed to me that just about everything else in the world was of higher importance to her than us. And it wasn't the first time we talked about it. Susan and I call these kinds of topics "scripts," because they are contentious issues that we address time and time again just like a script in a play or movie that you see again and again.

Knowing this topic was a script, I thought I'd disguise my accusation by taking full responsibility in saying that I've recently failed as a leader in our marriage because our relationship didn't seem to be a priority to her right then. I was hoping her response would be, "Honey, you're so right. I apologize. I'll try harder to put us first. Come here and let me give you a hug."

Instead, here's what I got: "You're right. You haven't been a loving leader lately. You've been impatient and uptight. You're not very fun to be around right now, and you're also right that I don't want to spend time with you." She went on to say that I may have been trying to be a loving leader, but it was clear that my heart was not in it.

My response? "Just forget it," I said. "Obviously I'm not a loving leader. No sense in writing a book about it when I can't even do it myself." Susan then butted in on my pity party and said, "No, that's why you should write this book. Share with people how hard it is and how you struggle to be a loving leader and what you're doing about it; how to love and lead through your struggles."

So, here I am. Still working, still striving to lead with love. Does all this mean my wife has no responsibility to make our relationship a priority even if I'm being a prickly porcupine? Of course not. But if I'm truly leading in our relationship with love, then she will most likely have a greater desire to do so.

My motives were not pure in my discussion with Susan. Why? Because my heart is not pure. Motive is fundamentally a heart issue. So, what is the heart? Yes, your physical heart is a muscle that pumps life-giving blood throughout your body. But the word *heart* has been used for thousands and thousands of years to describe the core of who you are, the "real you." It's the central command for all your thoughts, beliefs, desires, affections, conscience, convictions, emotions, and motives. Who you are, what you say, what you do, how you think, and what you feel are all ultimately impacted by the status of your heart.

Don't Follow Your Heart

So, should you just "follow your heart" as you date, in your marriage, while you work, as you socialize? No. At least not most of the time. That's because when most people say, "Follow your heart," they're really just saying, "Follow your feelings." And yes, feelings by themselves can sometimes lead you down a smooth road, but more often than not, they'll lead you on a road full of potholes and maybe even a fatal crash.

Think about it. How many times have you heard about a man divorcing his wife of many years, saying, "I don't feel respected by her. She's always nagging me and trying to change me"? How many women have you heard say, "I don't feel in love anymore" or "I'm just not happy"? They're leaving their husbands for men who "really listen, understand, and care."

And how many have left their jobs on a whim because they "felt" like starting a new business, which quickly went under? We live in a culture where people make major decisions solely in response to their feelings, regardless of who they hurt or what promises they break.

But Stephen and Alex Kendrick, in their book *The Love Dare*, say the problem with "following your heart," as most people define it, is that you are just chasing whatever feels right at the moment, even though it may not be right. It means throwing caution to the wind and pursuing your latest whim, even though it may not be logical. The Kendricks further note that "people forget that feelings and emotions are shallow, fickle, and unreliable."[1] They can fluctuate depending upon circumstances.

LEAD YOUR HEART

The Kendricks further suggest that instead of following your heart, you should lead your heart. They say, "You need to understand that your heart follows your investment."[2] In other words, your heart will follow whatever you pour your time, talent, and treasure into. If you pour most of your time into Facebook and Twitter, your thoughts and emotions will be there. If your talents and energy are focused completely on your job, a big part of you will reside there as well. If your treasure is used to accumulate cars, boats, and other stuff, that's where your desires and affections will be. "For where your treasure is, there your heart will be also," Jesus says.[3] The Kendricks say to lead your heart in four ways—check your heart, guard your heart, set your heart, and invest your heart.

1. Check Your Heart

A key to leading your heart is to constantly be aware of where it is. Where is your heart? If your motive for doing things is focused on "what's in it for me?" you will constantly gravitate toward things that reward yourself. If recognition is important to you, you will spend your time on things that will achieve that heartfelt need. If a plaque, pat on the back, or round of applause is what you're looking for, you might just seek to be chairman of the upcoming annual dinner at your company because you'll most likely get it there. And if being exalted means a lot to you, that will be an easy fix because you're not likely to get those accolades, awards, and applause from your spouse and kids. Think about it. When was the last time your child gave you a plaque that stated "To our awesome father, in recognition for dedicating your life to us"? Or when did you walk in the door, after a grueling day at work, and receive a standing ovation from your family? To lead your heart, you must first know where it is.

2. Guard Your Heart

When something unhealthy or wrong tempts your heart, you must guard your heart against that temptation.

Succumbing to temptation, simply put, is caving in to something because it will, at least temporarily, satisfy you.

All of us are tempted. The question is, what are we going to do with that temptation that constantly sneaks its way into our lives? A proverb says, "Above all else, guard your heart, for it is the wellspring of life."[4] When temptation calls our name and seduces us, rarely do we take a step back, look at it logically, and say, "Okay, I see this thing that is tempting me. Sure, it is exciting, it's fun, and will make me feel so good. But I'm not going to go there because it not only will hurt me in the long run but will deeply wound my wife and my children."

So, how then can we guard our hearts against being taken on a dangerous detour toward an affair, gambling, greed, workaholism, or pornography? We need to put guardrails in place that will keep us from veering off the road in our most important relationships.

The temptation of pornography is huge, and putting up a strong guardrail against it is vital. Porn is everywhere and is only a click away on your laptop or a touch away on your smartphone. But it's a beast that kills—kills the soul and ravages relationships. Porn creates unrealistic and false expectations for your sexual relationship with your spouse. It promotes the lie that relationships are all about getting instead of giving.

Another lie about pornography is this popular phrase: "I'll do it one more time, then I'll stop." But pornography is like a drug: some is never enough; you always need more and more and something stronger and stronger for the high to continue. As a result, soft porn leads to hard porn. And pornography often leads to an extramarital affair.

So, what should you do? Start by bringing to light what has been hidden in darkness by sharing your struggles with your spouse, pastor, or friend. Flee from it immediately and avoid pornography completely. Put your computer in a very public place in your house or get rid of it for a season of time. Upload software to filter out pornography. Never erase your computer history. Allow your spouse to hold you accountable and give her all your passwords.

Having traveled around the world, performed in front of millions of people, and spent countless nights alone in hotels, recording artist Michael W. Smith knows the importance of guarding his heart. "I'm really careful about what I look at on my computer and on the TV. I think those are always temptations. And then I think, the biggest thing is, who are your friends? Who are you walking with? Do you have a little 'band of brothers' who hold you accountable? I think we all need that, especially us men. We've gotta walk hand in hand with great friends who will hold us accountable. I think that's real key."[5]

Whatever the temptation might be, you and I are both just one decision away from giving up a lifetime relationship with our wife and children for a moment of pleasure. "Well," you might say, "my wife is as cold as ice. She does nothing for me. Getting her to make love with me is like pulling teeth.

This other woman makes me feel like a man; she really desires me, she makes me come alive! So I'd rather have a moment of pleasure than nothing at all." But most men who have gone down that road will tell you the temporary pleasure wasn't worth the long-term pain it caused to themselves and their family. And any man who denies this truth is flat-out living a lie. The better road to take is the one you are on, and the better choice is to repair the potholes in your relationship. More on this in our chapter on knowing your Method.

3. Set Your Heart

A leader sets the climate in the home. How? Let me illustrate. A thermostat regulates the temperature, while a thermometer reflects the temperature. In my home, if it's too hot, I can make it cooler simply by adjusting the thermostat. Likewise, if it's too cold, I can make it warmer. You can't do that with a thermometer. A thermometer simply reports the temperature but does nothing to regulate it.

So, are you a thermostat or a thermometer in your home? Too many parents, and especially fathers, are thermometers; they reflect their wife or child's mood. If Karen is a sweet and attentive wife, all is good. But if she's not, the hair on the back of her husband's neck starts to rise up. If David is behaving, then dad is fine. But if David is rebellious . . . well, you get the picture. But effective fathers should be thermostats, setting the climate of the household by how they react, or don't react, to the behavior of others in the family. They choose to be joyful when their spouse is hurtful. They choose to be calm when their child is out of control. And they choose to love when their child is unlovable. Easy to say, hard to do.

Bottom line? A father who leads his heart pushes aside what he wants to make himself happy and determines that he will do what's best for his family: to demonstrate patience, kindness, and self-control despite the heat in the house.

4. Invest Your Heart

When you invest in the stock market, in real estate, or in most anything, you get help from a trusted advisor, do your due diligence, explore your options, and then make a commitment by making the purchase or signing the contract. You're intentional about it. In the same way, be intentional about how you invest your heart. Be intentional about praising and encouraging your son or daughter every opportunity you can even though your child may not be performing to your expectations on the field or in the classroom. Be intentional about showing patience and kindness to your wife. Don't wait until you "feel like it." Do it today. If you need a guide by your side to show you how to do it, ask for help from a trusted friend and father who you admire.

Okay, so hopefully I've provided you with some thoughts on why you should lead your heart. But should you ever follow your heart? Well, yes. That is, if you're talking about not just your feelings, but all of your heart. And only if it jives with God's truth. And only if you know your ultimate motive and goal is to honor God.

Three Phases of Growth from Selfish to Selfless Motives

The more you lead your heart, the more pure in your motives you'll become; and the more pure in your motives you become, the more your capacity to love will grow. That is, our desire to humbly, selflessly serve and sacrifice increases as our motives become more pure. Most of us go through three phases of growth that have a big impact on our motives.

Phase 1

In phase one, our life is ruled by selfishness. It's where we are full of self. We want to be the greatest, the first. We want first choice, first place, first pick, first team, first class, first me! We want the seat of honor at the banquet. We want to be recognized in the program. Have you ever gotten down because your name wasn't mentioned during the presentation, especially after all your hard work? Did you silently shout out, "Hey, what about me? Look what I've done"? Like a dry sponge, we can be so self-absorbed that even if we squeeze it, not a bit of love flows out into the lives of others.

About 5 percent of the world population lives in the United States,[6] but about 25 percent of all economic activity occurs in our country.[7] That means we have much. But it also means we are big consumers. We can buy just about anything we want right now, so that our desires can be met right now. So what's the big deal? Well, that consumption way of thinking has also spilled over into our relationships. We've become "relationship consumers." Our underlying motive is often to use people to get something out of them for our selfish purposes and pleasures, then dispose of them. We consume others because we're selfishly focused on ourselves.

Here's a major problem with the consumption way of thinking. If all we do is consume, then things—and even people—will be digested, go through our system, and then ultimately be discarded. When that happens, we'll be hungry again for something more, something different to satisfy ourselves. Our demand will only increase. There will never be enough.

I'll confess. I'm a selfish person—born that way. It was especially apparent in my teens and twenties. At the time, I didn't think much about it; I just did what was best for me. I served on boards and sought appointments to key positions—all for recognition, to get my name in the limelight. It was all about me. I was self-absorbed. I also went to a lot of banquets. And do you know the first thing I would do when I sat down? I would look at the program not only to see if my name was in it as a table sponsor or speaker, but also to see if it was spelled correctly! Part of me is still stuck in this phase, but, thankfully, part of me is now in phase two.

Phase 2

In phase two, self-absorption is still present, but at least on the outside it doesn't appear to rule our lives. We let people get ahead of us in line, but we do it so that everyone will notice what we've done. We sit in the very back of the room, but we do it in hopes that someone will see us, tap us on the shoulder, and move us to the front of the room. We help the needy and feed the poor, but we do it so that others will see us and praise us. In this phase, we still struggle internally and have to squeeze love out of ourselves into the lives of others.

By the way, if you're thinking you're fooling your wife or kids, think again. You may not know this, but your wife and children are a bit like Superman. They seem to have some sort of X-ray vision. They have this uncanny ability to see right through you and into the depths of your heart. Whether they verbalize it or not, they know why you say or do what you do. They know your motive. They know whether you are genuine or not.

There have been many occasions where I've done the dishes. On the outside, it looked like I was doing a nice thing so that Susan could relax for a few minutes after dinner. But what she didn't know, at least initially, was why I was so eager to do so. My thinking went like this: *I'll do the dishes, she won't be so tired, and she'll see how much I really care about her well-being. Then, we'll get in bed, and the payoff will arrive. I'll have guaranteed reservations for making love.* It was all about getting, not giving.

By the way, Susan quickly caught on and we joked about it a lot. From then on, I'd say, "Honey, I'm going to do the dishes now, okaaaay?!" It was my private code letting her know that I'd like to make love later on. Did it work? Well, sometimes.

Phase 3

I'm learning that to truly love my wife and children, my motive must grow in purity. I must give selflessly, not selfishly; give without expectation of receiving anything in return. Notice I said, "grow in purity," because we can never achieve complete purity in this sense due to our selfish nature. Perfectly pure motives are forever elusive. But I'm always shooting for that goal. I'm striving for phase three.

Phase three is not perfection. No such thing. It's just where we, generally speaking, are satisfied with being last or being first, with being in the back or the front, with being noticed or being anonymous. We're satisfied because we have a deep desire within our hearts to love God, our families, and others and serve them wherever we are and in whatever circumstances we find ourselves. It's where we are so saturated with God and His love that it spills out into the lives of others.

Jeb Bush did amazing things as governor of our state and for families in Florida. He deserves many awards. But having known Jeb and served his administration in several ways, I know that awards are not something he cares much about. In fact, I remember asking him if Family First could honor him with a prestigious national award we give each year. He graciously declined. He doesn't do awards. He does what he does no matter what. He doesn't do it for the recognition; he does it out of conviction. Jeb's satisfaction comes from knowing he's helped and served others.

Several years ago, Cary Gaylord, chairman of the board of Family First, took a knife for someone named Mary. Many years earlier, Mary was diagnosed with a fatal kidney disease. But by the end of 2005, she started having great pain and was at the doorstep of death. She needed an immediate transplant. No compatible donor could be found from within her family. So, without hesitation, Cary stepped up to the plate, got tested, and bingo, found he was the perfect match. He selflessly gave what money could not buy: the gift of life. He underwent surgery, endured the risk and pain, and gave his kidney to his friend so she could live. What was the payback? What did he get out of it? Only the reward of knowing that he literally gave of himself to save the life of his friend.

I haven't given a kidney to save anyone's life. I wonder if I would. I would like to think so, but I haven't had to cross that road yet. But I can say that I'm growing a little bit in the purity of my motives. Being married for twenty-two years and having five children has had a way of humbling and stripping me of my self-focus and selfish motives. But, unfortunately, I haven't lost all of that selfishness even to this day. I suspect I'll have it for the rest of my life here on earth.

At least now, when I make most decisions, I constantly ask myself,

"What's my motive?"

"Why do I really want to do this?"

"Do I really want to give of myself or am I just
    trying to get something out of it?"

I had to ask this motive question many times before I decided to write this book. I mean, everyone is an author these days. Why do we need another book? Well, the truth of the matter is that we don't! But after thinking and praying about it for about a decade, I decided that my motive, though there are still traces of impurity, is somewhat pure. I do feel like there is an important message I want to share with you in this book that might help you in your life journey to better love and lead others.

What's Your Motive?

Stop and ask yourself, "What's my motive? Why do I help others?" Winston Churchill once said, "We make a living by what we get, but we make a life by what we give."[8] Each of us needs to ask ourselves, "Am I a serving or self-serving leader? Am I living my life to give or to get?"

Tony Dungy knows just how important our motives are. Here's his take: "You can be a leader and have the wrong motivation and people will follow you. But eventually, if you don't have the proper motive, you're going to make decisions that are going to be wrong, that will be bad for those you lead, whether it's your family or your team. You're going to lead in the wrong direction if you don't have the right motive."[9]

Norm Miller, founder of Interstate Batteries, told me that when he was younger, he often had the wrong motives: "I was real selfish. I ran over people. My natural instinct was about looking after myself. For me, it was all about getting. But two DUIs, back to back, made me realize that I needed to treat others as I wanted to be treated. It showed me the importance of valuing others. The ultimate in life is loving, and loving is giving."[10]

In every episode of the television show *Law and Order: SVU*, the special victims unit of the NYPD is searching for evidence so they can track down the perpetrator of the crime. They often find that evidence in the fingerprints on things that have been left behind, the fingerprints of someone who took something away from another. As fathers, we can leave a legacy of fingerprints behind that provide evidence of what we *took* from relationships, or we can leave a legacy of "love-prints" behind as evidence that we *gave* and *gave* and *gave* to our family and to others.

What about you? What are you living your life for? Are you leading your heart toward more selfless motives? The condition of your heart will play a major role in determining whether your children will follow you only with their head out of strict obedience to the law you've laid down, or whether they'll follow you with their whole heart, because they desire to do so. If they only follow the strict letter of the law for fear of consequences, then when they leave your parental jurisdiction for college or a career, they'll most likely follow the lead and influence of others who won't care so much about them. But, if they have a heartfelt desire to follow you because you have been a loving leader with a Phase 3 heart, then they'll carry that desire with them as they move to another place or another stage in their lives.

It's such an encouragement to watch Susan with two of our girls who are now in college. It seems that just about every day they are calling her to ask for her opinion about something. They call for advice on how to deal with a difficult situation with a friend. They call to get coaching on how to handle relationships with young men. They even text her pictures of clothes and shoes to get her feedback. And sometimes, they just call Susan to chat. But all of that didn't just happen. It took many years of love for Susan to earn the right to lead them. And while my girls don't seek me out for my advice in the shoe department, I'm grateful that I'm able to encourage and coach them a bit on some other things.

Motive is a heart issue. So lead your heart and strive for the purest motives. As you do, you'll greatly expand your capacity to love and lead your children today and many years into the future.

HUDDLE UP AND ASK YOUR CHILD:

1 Do you think giving is better than getting? Why?

2 Do you think people think more about themselves or others? Why?

3 Have you ever seen me act selfishly? When?

4 Who is the most giving person you know? Why do you say he or she is so giving?

KNOW YOUR METHOD

How Can I Better Love My Family?

To love means loving the unlovable.

—G. K. Chesterton

The porcupine is a very vocal animal. It has a wide variety of calls, including moans, grunts, coughs, shrieks, wails, and whines. (That sounds a lot like some of us men!) But the most recognizable feature of this rodent is its quills, which can number as many as thirty thousand. The quills are hairs with barbed tips on the ends. The porcupine has quills on all parts of its body, with the exception of its stomach. The longest quills are on its rear end.

When irritated or threatened, the porcupine stamps its feet, growls, hisses, and places his snout between his forelegs and spins around, presenting its rear to the other animal. If the porcupine hits the animal with its quills, the quills become embedded and can cause enormous pain.[1]

But one of the most interesting facts about porcupines is that when you calm them, you can actually pet them if you use the right method. You have to do it front to back in a very thoughtful fashion. Any kind of carelessness can lead to piercing pain.

So when I come home and walk through the door really cranky, stomping my feet and hissing, with my prickly quills sticking up, my wife instantly sees it and whispers, "Uh-oh, the porcupine is home." At that point, she has three choices, and only one of them will draw me closer to her. She can prod with her words by saying something like "What's your problem?" But that just makes me growl more. She can also run from me, the porcupine. But the problem with that is the porcupine is still in the house. Or, she can hug me by gently putting her arms around me and drawing me close. So she hugs me, even though I'm unlovable, and even risks hurting herself, because a hug is what this porcupine needs. So love the porcupine, hug and pet the porcupine, even though you risk getting hurt. In the end, it will draw you and your spouse closer.

You may be thinking, *That all sounds good, but what do porcupines and my relationship with my wife have to do with fatherhood?* Everything. If you are married, the most important thing you can do for your children is to have a healthy marriage. The best way to love and lead your kids is to first love and lead your spouse, even when he or she is a porcupine. I'd like to share with you several truths for your marriage that will help you do just that.

TRUTHS FOR YOUR MARRIAGE

Let's face it. All of us are porcupines from time to time, and the key is to have the right method in our marriage to deal with each other's irritability. Our society thinks compatibility is the key to a successful marriage. That's wrong. Flourishing marriages are built on conflict resolution—how to work through issues and come out on the other side loving each other more. Here are four important truths to remember as you strive to love and lead your spouse through those prickly and precarious times in your relationship.

Truth #1: Your Spouse Is Not the Enemy

First, remember that your spouse is not the enemy. I repeat: your spouse is not the enemy. Let me say that again: your spouse is not the enemy. Have you heard it said, before marriage, opposites attract; after marriage, opposites attack? What was once appealing may now be annoying.

Before Susan and I got married, more than twenty-two years ago, she was attracted to me for my decisiveness and strong will. As the years have gone by, those qualities sometimes bother her. At this stage in her life, she's looking for more empathy and understanding, not a husband who is always grabbing the reigns and cracking the whip. Before marriage, I was attracted to Susan for her creativity and do-everything attitude; now that creative bent and busyness can annoy me. I want more order in the house. I want more of her time and attention.

So, what should we do? Have a standoff for the rest of our life together? Of course not. We should remember and appreciate those qualities we first saw in our spouse. At the same time, we can share with them that we are in a different season of life where we desire more patience, kindness, or _____ (you fill in the blank). We also need to be willing to work on changing some things in our own behavior to meet the wishes of our spouse at this stage in our relationship.

Please note that the point here is not to create unrealistic expectations for our spouses; we don't have the power to change them. Also, realize that it may be a long process for the change to take place, if it even happens at all. The person you loved so much in the beginning of your relationship is still there. You just have to look past the quirks that you find annoying to uncover the qualities that your spouse has to offer.

Truth #2: Your Spouse Is on Your Team

The second truth is that you and your wife are on the same team. See if these scenarios sound familiar: He's having a blast with his buddies on the golf course; she's back at home cleaning the house. Or she's out having fun with her friends; he's back home mowing the yard. "I'm always the bad guy," she exclaims. "How come you get to go play with the kids and I'm the one who always gets stuck disciplining them?" Or, he says, "You just got a new couch, so why can't I spend a measly hundred bucks on some new fishing gear?"

Husbands and wives can sometimes find themselves keeping a marital scorecard. They keep track of who spends more, disciplines more, does the dishes more, cleans more, mows more, and works more. If couples aren't careful, they can become bitter and resent the other for not helping enough or for having more fun. If not addressed, a husband and wife can even feel like enemies.

So, if you find yourself keeping score, what should you do? First, remember this key thought: you were designed to *complete* each other, not *compete* with each other. Marriage is the ultimate team sport, and marriages only work well when husbands and wives remember that they're on the same team.

Second, we know that love is not jealous or selfish. Love is all about giving. So a loving wife knows when her husband needs support, and she helps him. She encourages her man. A loving husband sacrifices and gives time to his wife when he senses she is overwhelmed. He cherishes his woman and ensures her physical and emotional health. He encourages her.

Third, as you go through your day ask yourself, "Is this a good decision not only for me but also for my mate?" And, "Is this something that's going to help our team or hurt it?" Teamwork in marriage requires a selfless, sacrificial, and giving spirit.

Truth #3: Your Tongue Has Remarkable Power

The third truth I want you to remember is that you have remarkable power right under your nose. The power of the tongue is so great that it's capable of discouraging or encouraging, hurting or healing, tearing down or building up. Think about it. If you didn't have a tongue, you couldn't speak and you'd eliminate most conflict in your relationships.

But you probably do have a tongue. So, what do you do when your spouse takes aim at you and starts to fire a verbal assault? Fire right back, right? Well, that's our instinct, but when we lead with love we receive the "friendly fire," and don't pull the verbal trigger, even though everything in us says, "Let it rip!" Sometimes responding with a gentle answer like, "It makes me sad that you feel that way," or not saying anything at all, is the best response.

The tongue is a wild animal. You need to chain it, tame it, and train it. Train it to breathe life into those you love.

Truth #4: You Must Love Your Unlovable Spouse

The fourth truth to remember is that one of the hardest things for you to do is to love unlovable people, especially your spouse. It's easy to love them when they are kind, sweet, and lovable, but we must love them when they are unlovable; love them no matter what.

Remember, when we got married each of us made a choice to love our spouse for life, for better or worse. We made a choice to love them even when they're unlovable. When I speak, I often illustrate this point of unconditional love by having the men in the audience turn to their wives and repeat after me:

> Honey, I love you when you don't wear makeup. I love you when you have PMS. I love you when you go shopping and max out our credit card. I love you when you tell me to put down the remote. I love you no matter what!

Wives get their turn too. I ask them to turn to their husbands and repeat the following:

Honey, I love you when you have gas in the house. I love you when you snore. I love you when you don't put the toilet seat down. I love you when you get lost and won't ask for directions. I love you no matter what!

Of course, they all get a few chuckles out of it, but they get the point that loving your spouse no matter what, means no matter what. And, by the way, love is not dependent on the person being loved receiving that love, because remember, love is unconditional. It's not an "if you do this, I'll do that" kind of thing, it's "I'll do this regardless of what you do." So love the porcupine, no matter what. Even when it hurts.

As a husband, you need to have the right methodology for dealing with your wife when she becomes a porcupine from time to time. And if you lead your heart, as we discussed in our chapter on Motive, and lead with love in this area of resolving conflicts graciously, she'll more than likely return the favor. And you will find your love for each other deepening.

TRUTHS ABOUT TIME

Just as we have a method for loving and leading our spouse well, we must also have a method for demonstrating our love to our children.

Do your children know you love them? How do they know? Well, if you want an honest answer, all you have to do is ask them. That's what I did with my kids when they were younger, before Hannah and Grant joined our family. I first asked Megan, "Megan, how do you know I love you?"

"Because you tickle me," she said.

So I said, "What if my hands were tied behind my back and I couldn't tickle you? Then how would you know that I love you?"

She responded, "Because you spend time with me."

Then I asked Emily, "Emily, how do you know that I love you?"

"Because you say so," she said.

"Well, what if my lips were zipped together and I couldn't say so? Then how would you know that I love you?"

She smiled and shouted, "Because you play with me!"

My son Marky was next. Anyone who knows Marky knows that he has always been a man of few words. "Marky, how do you know I love you?" I asked.

He looked at me, shrugged his shoulders, and with a grin said, "I don't know."

That's my boy!

Woven into each one of their answers (and Marky would give a similar response to the girls' answers if pushed) is a common thread that gives us a better understanding of what kids value: time. You've heard it said before that kids spell *love* with another four-letter word—T.I.M.E. And not only do they value your time, but it's one of the most valuable things you possess, because, unlike money and things that have finite value and can be replaced, time has infinite value and can never be replaced. People often say, "Time is money." I say, "Time is love." Spending time—not money—with our children is one of the best indicators to them that we love them. Spend more time with them.

We want to believe the myth that all we need is *quality* time with our kids. But, our kids need *quantity* time. Using the right method in how we spend time with our kids translates to loving and leading them well. Have you ever heard your child say to you, "Dad, we have played way too much. Why don't you go back to work and get some things done?" Of course not. They want quantity time.

But you might say, "I just don't have time." Well, I would suggest that there's no such thing as not having time. When we say, "I don't have time," what we're really saying is that we don't choose to make certain things a priority right now, or there's something else we'd rather be doing. When Marky was a little boy, one Saturday morning he showed me his ball and glove and said, "Dad, let's play baseball." Of course, since I'm Mr. Family Guy, I said, "Sure, son." Right? Wrong. No, I said, "I don't have time right now. I'm fixing the toilet. Just give me a few minutes." Well, the minutes turned into hours and when I was ready that afternoon to play ball, my son said, "No thanks, Dad."

Think about all the demands on your schedule and take a look at the things you spend the most time on. The truth is, we make time for the things we want to make time for. But that isn't always necessarily what we should make time for. Starting today, make it a priority to set aside time for what's ultimately important: your child.

Do you know what your kids will remember about their childhood? Will they cherish the memories of the Xbox, PS3, or cell phone you bought them? No. Instead, they will remember you taking the time to cook pancakes for them and have meals with them. They will remember camping with you, wrestling with you, and building a fort together in the backyard. They will remember mom writing those special notes for their lunchboxes, cheering for them at their games, and having a make-believe tea party with them. Our children won't reminisce about big events and big-ticket items. Rather, their hearts will be warmed by memories of the love, care, and companionship you showed them day to day. Those are the things that will make a lasting impression they will carry with them into the future.

MEMORABLE MONUMENTS

Have you ever visited Washington, DC, and seen the Washington Monument? Why was it built? So that you and I would remember an important person and an important event. And how was it built? It was built with a lot of hard work so that generations and generations can come see it and remember.

Our children need us to build lasting monuments in their lives. I call them "memorable monuments." Memorable monuments are things you do with and for your children that create lasting, loving memories. These monuments are not always some big, planned, lengthy event or activity. They're small monuments you choose to build into the foundation of their lives day by day.

Build Memorable Monuments *with* Your Child

The next time you walk in the door from work and the kids meet you wanting your full attention, instead of telling them you're going upstairs to change before you play with them, stop, drop, and listen. Stop when you come in the door, drop to your knees, listen to them, hug them, play with them. As Dr. Seuss said in his book title, let them *Hop on Pop* for a few minutes. They'll be bored with you after sixty seconds anyway! But a monument will be built.

It helped me to have all of my kids' sports and school activities on my calendar, even if I couldn't make all of them, so that I could make sure to work as much of it into my day as possible. Once right after a business lunch, I had about half an hour before my next appointment. I saw on my calendar that my daughter Megan was cheering at a school pep rally.

So I made a detour to the school to watch her for just fifteen minutes before returning to the office. I saw her; she saw me. We both smiled. I left and went back to work. A small monument was planted.

And, every month, on each of my kids' birthday dates, I tried to take them somewhere they wanted to go. For example, Emily's birthday is on the tenth of the month. So on the tenth of each month, it was her turn. It might have been something as simple as going bike riding or getting hot chocolate before school. Something she wanted to do. Did I do it consistently? No. But the point is, I made a real effort. It was another memorable monument. Who knows, when they have kids of their own, maybe they'll say to their children, "Grandpa used to take me to do something fun on my birthday date each month, and I'm going to do the same thing with you." It's another memorable monument.

Tampa Bay Buccaneers general manager Mark Dominik, husband to Amy and father of three young children, and I were speaking on the phone Saturday afternoon, July 30, as he and his four-year-old son Davis were driving home from the Buccaneers training camp. "Davis and I are on our way home from our morning training camp," Mark said with an air of excitement in his voice. "I packed up his backpack, some of his toys, and his blanket, and we went to work for three to four hours. We also had lunch with some of the players. I want my son to be a part of my work life and I take him to work a lot, especially on Saturdays. It's an important tradition for us to have those Saturday workdays." Even though Mark's calendar is filled to the brim every year when NFL training camps start, he is committed to building a memorable monument with his son.

Mark is laying the foundation for memorable monuments in his young daughter's life too. "I also started a tradition with my nineteen-month-old daughter, Emerson," Mark shared. "We started doing a daddy-daughter walk. It's when I come home from work and we just walk up and down the sidewalk in front of our house and talk. I want to keep doing that and communicate like that with her as she gets older. I want her to remember that we always did this together."[2]

A few years back I was with a friend whose high school daughter made homecoming court. I asked him if he was looking forward to escorting her on the football field at halftime. He replied that he had a big trip and wouldn't be there. I said, "John, if you are not there, she will never forget it. And, if you are there, she will never forget it. Which memory of you would you like her to have?" Well, after I put him on that guilt trip, John cancelled his trip. He was probably with his daughter for only twenty minutes that night. But he built a memorable monument that neither will ever forget.

As our children get older, it seems to become more challenging to drive those monuments into the foundation of their lives, but it is no less important. Especially during the teen years, availability is the key. When it comes to spending time with our kids, we need to say yes every possible time because anyone with teens knows that those opportunities may not come as often as they used to.

When they're home for spring break, for example, I try to go in really early to work so that I can get home earlier, since they don't even wake up until 11:00 a.m.! When they get home late at night, Susan is always available for them because that's when they want to talk about their evening, their friends, their challenges. When they want to grab a burger at midnight, I gladly jump in the car and take them.

During those teen years, I've also found that searching for and finding that "one thing" is important. It's that one thing they like to do and will do with you. For Megan, it's shopping. For Emily, it's soup and salad at a nearby restaurant and then an old movie together. For Hannah, it's jogging. For Marky, it's hunting. For Grant, it's camping. That one thing they like to do with you will very likely become a memorable monument that they'll remember well into the future.

BUILD MEMORABLE MONUMENTS *FOR* YOUR CHILD

As leaders in our homes, just as we should build memorable monuments *with* our children, we should also build those monuments *for* our children. Once again, you are taking a small amount of your precious commodity, your time, to show love to your children. Here are a few things to think about as you build those monuments for your children.

Pillow Talk

Do you ever feel like things are moving so fast in your daily life that all you can do is yell out basic instructions as your children fly by: "Did you brush your teeth?" "Did you feed the dog?" "Please don't provoke your brother." "Don't forget your geography project." "When is your orthodontist appointment?" "Drive safely and call me when you get there." "How could you forget your homework?"

As our children grow older, it seems our days get busier with each passing year. It was during one of these busy seasons that Susan began to feel as if all communication with our children was becoming instructional or disciplinary. She would often drop them all off at school after a rushed morning and drive away pining for more tender moments and kind words with them. At other times she would think about the many good things they had done that she hadn't praised them for because she was too busy reminding and instructing. Leaks began sprouting in her communication with them and relationships were dampened.

The busyness of these different seasons of life was sadly blowing away opportunities for Susan to encourage our children. It was time for a change. Somehow she needed to bring her relationship with our children away from the gusts of daily living that pull them away from each other and into the calm and encouraging eye of the hurricane. And so one day after observing our daughter put into practice something Susan had been coaching her to do—not lash back at her sister when provoked—Susan wrote to her. It so happened on this particular morning Susan and two of our daughters were in the car on the way to school. To praise our daughter for not lashing back in front of the other child would have belittled the one provoking, further establishing the sibling rivalry. Instead, Susan said nothing but later wrote a note of praise and left it on her bed. Well, our daughter loved finding the note and Susan was convicted by the need to write words of encouragement more often. As the children got older, the notes got more complicated and lengthy and Susan often wondered what they thought in return.

About this time, my sister-in-law, Karen Merrill, shared a summer project she had done with her daughter. They wrote back and forth to one another in a spiral-bound notebook. This would become our solution. So we got journals for each of our kids and started writing notes to them, placing the journals on their pillows whenever we had written a new letter to them. They did the same for us. It was so encouraging that Susan developed the Pillow Talk journal for parents and kids. What a great way to build memorable monuments for your children.

Lunchbox Notes

Another way to uplift our children is to slip them a note in their lunchbox. Susan and I found that just simply letting them know we were thinking of them encouraged them through the day. Not sure what to write? How about: "I love you," "I'm proud of you," "Have a great day," or "Hope your test goes well"? You can even surprise them with a "Let's go for ice cream after school" note.

Letters to My Children

In our chapter on knowing your makeup, I shared how you can validate your children's identity and gifts in a letter. Another thing I've done for my children is to memorialize, in writing, the most important things I tried to instill in them as they were growing up. Three of our five children are now in college or working. Before they left our nest, there were four things Susan and I taught them and always want them to remember. Here is generally what I penned to each of them.

- **Remember who you are—your identity.** So many people spend much of their lives trying to determine their identity. They constantly struggle and attempt to create and re-create their identity by how they act, how they look, what they wear, what they drive, where they live, and what they've got because they don't have any idea who they are and how valuable they are. You don't have to do that because God has given you your identity and value. You were created and chosen by God. You are wonderfully made.
- **Remember why you are here—your purpose.** In my younger years, it was really important to me to get the approval of other people. For example, when I spoke publicly, I was always thinking things like, *Do they like what I'm saying? Do they like the way I'm saying it? What*

do they think about me? I was focused on me and was seeking the approval of others. Once I learned to take the focus off me, fear of what other people thought and fear of making mistakes was replaced with freedom to be the person God created me to be. God does not want us to seek the approval, accolades, and applause of others. He desires for us to look only to the audience of one person for everything, God Almighty, and to do everything to please, glorify, and honor Him alone. Your purpose in life is to glorify God and enjoy Him forever.

• **Remember how you should live—your life.** God tells us that the most important thing we can do is to love Him and love others. Jesus also says, "If you love me, you will obey what I command."[3] One of His commands is to read and meditate on His Word.[4] As you continue on your life journey, you will be making more and more decisions that will profoundly influence and impact you for the rest of your life here on earth. The Bible will provide the wisdom you need to make decisions that honor God.

• **Remember what God has promised you— your reward.** God loves you, and He has plans to prosper you, to give you hope and a future. God has plans to bless you and richly reward you for what you have done and what you will do for His glory here on earth.

THE REWARDS OF BUILDING
MEMORABLE MONUMENTS

So, when you build those memorable monuments with your children, do you just get memories? No. Time together does at least three things. First, it grows "heart relationships" between you and your children—a deep connection with your children that will withstand the test of time and storms of life. So when things get tough in your life, in their lives, or in your relationship, those monuments of time will be the glue that holds you both together.

Second, time together creates teachable moments. When you're hanging out together, they'll learn just by watching how you walk in your life. They'll also learn by listening.

Third, as I mentioned earlier, it's time together with our children that demonstrates our love for them. If they know that we truly love them and have their best interests at heart, they'll be much more likely to follow us. We'll have earned the right to lead them.

The late humorist Erma Bombeck wrote a column warning parents to cherish the childhood years, because in the blink of an eye they'll be gone. "Imagine . . . ," she said, "washing [clothes] only once a week . . . Having your teeth cleaned without a baby on your lap. No PTA meetings. No car pools. No blaring radios . . ." "Think about it," she continued. "No more Christmas presents out of toothpicks and library paste. No more sloppy oatmeal kisses. No more tooth fairy.

No giggles in the dark . . . Only a voice crying, 'Why don't you grow up?' and the silence echoing, 'I did.'"[5]

So that you can start building memorable monuments with and for your children, will you try something for your children, just for today? Just for today, tell your kids: I'll forget about my to-do list and take you to the park. I will silence the cell phone, turn off the computer, and have a tea party with you. Just for today, I will cancel my golf game and throw the football with you in the backyard. I will skip my favorite TV show and snuggle beside you for hours. Just for today I will let you stay up late so we can sit outside, gaze at the moon, and count the stars. Just for today, I will think about the fathers who no longer have their children, and I will be grateful I have you, just for today.

Just like your computer, you have a basic operating system that gives you the ability to love. But in order to expand your capacity to love, you need to have the right method of populating your "heart drive" with applications of love for it to be of any practical use. Adding these applications of memorable monuments to your drive may be just what you need to create a loving relationship, and a leading relationship, as a dad.

HUDDLE UP AND ASK YOUR CHILD:

1 How do you know I love Mom?

2 What is one of your favorite memories with me growing up?

3 What is one thing we have never done that you would like to do with me?

KNOW YOU'RE A MODEL

What Should I Model to My Children?

*Role modeling is the most basic
responsibility of parents. Parents are
handing life's scripts to their children,
scripts that in all likelihood will be acted
out for the rest of the children's lives.*
—Stephen R. Covey

W hy don't you talk to me the way you talk to your Family First supporters?" It was an unexpected question my wife shot over the bow of my ship in response to my speaking harshly to her. It was one of those penetrating questions that hit me right between the eyes.

I realized very quickly that I was speaking unkindly. That was apparent. I also knew that when I responded honestly, it would reveal something about me, maybe a truth I didn't want to see. It was one of those moments on my journey where I was on a stretch of rocky path that had the potential to trip me up. You see, for some reason, I had come to think that because Susan had been my wife for more than two decades, my closest companion and confidant, I had a special license to say anything I wished, in whatever tone I wished, when I was around her. I mean, I share my deepest thoughts and secrets with Susan. So why shouldn't I feel comfortable just being me, saying what's on my mind? Well, therein lies the problem. I was just being me, and it wasn't pretty. That wasn't the end, though.

Somewhere within my answer to her question there was an even more compelling truth I needed to explore in the deep waters of how I relate daily to those around me, especially with my family. Maybe I'm not always "me" around my friends and the people I work with. Maybe I'm sometimes nicer to them, especially with my words. The Author of Wisdom once said, "What comes out of the mouth proceeds from the heart."[1] So that one little question from Susan revealed an underlying heart condition that I need to continually address. Now, I'd like to think that this episode was an exception, rather than a rule in my life. I really do strive to live a model life where my walk matches my talk, and where my walk and talk are consistent in all areas of my life, private and public, personal and professional.

What about you? If the curtain were pulled back on your home life and personal relationships and people saw the real you, what would they see? Based on your words and actions, would they recognize you as the same person everywhere you went—at work, at school, at the store, at the gym, at the club, at church? Most importantly, who would they see in your home?

CONSISTENCY IS KEY

Most of us, in small or big ways, live compartmentalized lives. We have our home life, work life, church life, social life, and online life. Some of us, you could say, have almost nine lives. And we often live as though each of these lives is an island unto itself. We are one person with our family, another person with our friends, and still another person at work. We praise our friends and put down our family. We slap our clients on the back and slap our spouse in the face, hopefully only figuratively. The way we speak and behave in each area of our lives is sometimes very different.

Let's say you never look your boss in the eye and always mumble one-word answers to his questions. You probably wouldn't be working very long at that job, would you? Now, think of the way you interact with your spouse. When your wife speaks to you, do you avoid eye contact? When your wife asks questions, do you get annoyed and snippy? We often treat others better than we treat our own family members. But that's not the way it should be. We weren't wired to live like that. We were put together to act consistently, to live with one native language of love.

There are some who are in significant places of leadership who clearly understand how vital, but at the same time how difficult, it is to live consistently. Michael Ducker, COO and President, International, FedEx Express told me, "We all face the challenge of being consistent in our behavior in all areas of life."[2]

J. Wayne Huizenga Jr., chairman of Rybovich Marina and part owner of the Miami Dolphins, also addressed the challenge of consistency with me. "Am I nicer sometimes to a customer I'm courting to do a one-million-dollar refit for their yacht than I am to my spouse? Absolutely. So, how do I battle that? It's a struggle. I try to be intentional and treat them all the same. The same standard should apply at work and at home with my wife and kids, regardless of whether I'm tired. I need to keep my customer service hat on even when I am at home. If you love everyone, rather than just trying to turn it on for certain individuals, it becomes second nature. Love is an important part of leadership. I try to lead with love."[3]

Wayne isn't alone. All of us face the consistency challenge, including Dan Cathy, president of Chick-fil-A. "I camp out with Chick-fil-A customers before restaurant grand openings," Dan shared with me. "I've done over a hundred campouts. The first one hundred customers get to eat at Chick-fil-A for free for a year. I remind everybody at the campouts that you better watch it because when you've been up all night, you tend to lose your patience with others. Sure enough, I came home to my wife after having been up all night long. She made a comment to me, and I gave her a response in a tone that was not exactly what she was expecting. And so she walked over and pointed her index finger at me and said, 'Look, you can go around camping with customers if you want to all night, but you need to remember that your number one customer is still waiting for you when you get home.'"[4]

When retail millionaire J. C. Penney turned ninety-five, he said, "My eyesight may be getting weaker, but my vision is increasing."[5] As I look at my laptop screen, with my eyes now boasting 1.75 reading glasses, I can also confirm that my eyesight is getting worse but, like J. C., my vision is getting much, much better. And as my vision sharpens, I am seeing more clearly how this fragmented living impacts our lives in a negative way.

Compartmentalization hinders our relationships and creates conflict with others—conflict between friends, coworkers, parents and children, husbands and wives. We use words that tear down our children at home but build up friends at social gatherings; we have strategic plans at work but no goals for our kids at home; we generously serve coffee and donuts to others in church but forget to help our spouse with the dishes at home; we write books about love and leadership but neglect to apply it in our own lives!

In Florida, we have a lot of chameleons. These little guys look kind of like the Geico lizard. They change their color in different environments in order to blend in and protect themselves. We often operate the same way these little lizards do, and I call this behavior the "chameleon phenomenon." I think all of us have a bit of chameleon in us; some just have more than others.

As I mentioned previously, by and large, our children can see right through us. They know if we are the real deal or not. They need a consistent example to follow. Consistency is key in fatherhood.

UNDERSTANDING THE PRINCIPLE
OF SOWING AND REAPING

To be that consistent example for our children to follow, we need to understand the principle of sowing and reaping.

Have you ever planted a garden at home? When my kids were young, we planted gardens with green beans, corn, carrots, and tomato seeds. So, if you plant tomato seeds, what do you get? You get tomatoes, right? If you plant green bean seeds, you get green beans. You reap what you sow. In the same way, the seeds you plant in your relationships determine what you'll get in return. Do you want your children to be patient, kind, and respectful to you? Then sow seeds of patience, kindness, and respect to them. Want your spouse to be understanding, loving, and loyal? Then sow those same seeds yourself.

One night after my daughters were arguing, I asked one of them, "Emily, why can't you and your sister just be nice to each other?" Her response? "Dad, haven't you ever noticed that when you and Mom get along, we all get along?" Ouch! That hurts; but she's right. When my wife and I are short, harsh, and argumentative, our kids are too. When my wife and I are treating each other with patience, kindness, and respect, our kids seem to get along much better. You've probably heard the expression "Children learn more from what's caught than taught." In other words, you reap what you sow.

An important point to remember relating to this concept of reaping and sowing is that there's no quick harvest. If a farmer plants tomato seeds on Monday, he doesn't go out on Tuesday and pick them. There's always a time lag between sowing and reaping. As we plant seeds in our kids' lives, just remember that the harvest may not come for many months, and sometimes, many years. So keep sowing.

Our sowing will have a lot to do with our children's core convictions and beliefs. What we model to our children will have a great influence on what they think of themselves, what they think about their purpose in life, and how they view others. Our sowing will also influence how they view the world. An involved parent will, more likely than not, have children who have their same bent morally, financially, environmentally, politically, and vocationally.

While your children are not robots, you should mold and train them. Ask yourself: What characteristics do I want my children to exhibit as young men or young women? Do I want them to be patient or impatient? Do I want them to be kind or cranky? I know, these are obvious ones. But what about these: Do I want my children to have an excitement for the outdoors or a focus on doing things indoors? Do I want them to dress conservatively or with the newest fashion? Do I want them to vote and be active in the governmental process or stay away from politics? Do I want them to be musically inclined or sports inclined? You get the picture. And, by the way, most of these are not either/or; they can be both/and. The point is, whatever you desire those characteristics to look like, do them yourself. Again, you reap what you sow.

Here's a word of warning. If you are modeling things for your children because you want to look good to your friends and neighbors, or because you want your child to be a superstar you can brag about, or to make yourself feel good about yourself, or so you can live the life you didn't have through them, then you are barking up the wrong tree. That's a tree of selfishness and self-gratification. You should be having those desires for your children so that they'll be equipped to fulfill their purpose in life.

Mark Twain said, "Few things are harder to put up with than the annoyance of a good example."[6] I confess. I sometimes look at other fathers and get a bit annoyed. *Look at how his children hang on his every word*, I ponder. *Look at how much fun his kids are having with him. They're all laughing.* I see how well their children are doing—the grades they make, the teams they make, the manners they have—and start pulling my head back into my shell. Then I become very introspective and start focusing on my own mistakes and failures. Now, when I do that, I realize two things. First, I realize that things are often not what they seem. All fathers struggle. All fathers have failures. Second, I realize that I need to use their example, not to pull me back, but to propel me forward; not to retreat to a pity party, but to fight toward the goal of becoming an All Pro Dad.

A WORTHY MODEL

You've heard it time and time again: "Be a good role model." But you've probably heard it most in the context of an athlete, coach, celebrity, or other high-profile person who talks publicly to teens about staying in school, not having premarital sex, and not drinking, doing drugs, or smoking. So what's it got to do with being a dad? Everything. When you truly love your children, you will do what's best for them no matter what it costs you personally. For their sakes, you'll sacrifice anything, even your life. One of the best things you can do as a dad is to strive to live a model life that is worthy for your children to follow.

As I shared with you in the chapter on fatherhood fundamentals, by virtue of being a parent, you are a leader and therefore have followers you influence, namely your children. And because you influence your children, you are a role model. Remember, whether positively or negatively, we are all under the influence of others, and we all influence others. Someone is on the receiving end of everything you say and do. You have a great opportunity to influence your children.

Some would say they are not role models. In a Nike television commercial, former NBA player Charles Barkley states: "I am not a role model. I am not paid to be a role model. I am paid to wreak havoc on the basketball court. Parents should be role models. Just because I dunk a basketball doesn't mean I should raise your kids."[7]

Barkley is correct that parents should be role models and raise their kids. But he is wrong in saying he is not a role model. Whether he likes it or not, Charles Barkley is a role model. Again, it may be positive or negative, but we are all under the influence of others, and we all influence others. And, as a father, you are influencing your children all the time. They are always watching you.

FLIGHT PLAN FOR THE MODEL FATHER

Building model airplanes was a passion of mine growing up. Whether it was a Mustang P-51 fighter or a B-17 bomber, gluing all of the parts of the models together during my playtime on Saturdays was fun. After the final decal was placed on the planes, I proudly placed them on my dresser. I got a sense of satisfaction from building these things. As I grew older, my passion for building planes grew into a passion for flying planes. At the age of nineteen during my freshman year at college, I decided I wanted to become a pilot, so I went for it.

Learning about flying will provide a framework that will help you learn how to father well. So, for the remainder of this chapter, I'd like to develop a fatherhood flight plan that will provide you with a clear route to take in raising your children as a model father. Let's start with pilot training.

Pilot Training

When you train to be a pilot, you have to go through many hours of ground school and flight training. You learn by studying the books, but you also learn by flying the plane with a qualified instructor. The end goal of that instruction is for you to fly solo.

Maybe you had a father involved in your life growing up who not only told you but also showed you what being a model dad is all about. If that's the case, perhaps I can just give you a refresher course so that you'll be even more proficient in your flight as a father.

On the other hand, what if you've only received minimal instruction, or maybe none at all? Maybe you never knew your father. Maybe you did but he wasn't there, physically or emotionally, for you. You were there. You were ready for the training, but he never showed up. But, as tough as it may be, you can't just blame your father, have a victim mentality, follow the same course, and believe you don't have the instruments to be a great dad. Instead, even if you've been flying in the wrong direction as a father for many years, this is your opportunity to establish a new flight plan as a dad and create a new direction for your children and future generations of your family.

A pilot in training must remember that everything a pilot does should be done for his passengers. A pilot's mission is to care for his passengers and get them to their ultimate destination. Do you remember our mission as fathers? It's to love and lead our families. We must love and lead our children well and bring them to the place where they, in turn, will love and lead their children and others well.

A pilot also learns in his training that he must rely on instruments to get to his destination. He cannot rely on his own senses. One of the most important instruments of aeronautical navigation is the magnetic compass. Virtually everything that flies, from a Piper Cub to a Boeing 747, has a magnetic compass mounted to the windshield or instrument panel. Why? Because it can be used just about anywhere in the world. Also, it's the most reliable thing in the aircraft, since it uses no power or advanced technology. In the same way, as fathers we can't just rely on our own senses or feelings; we've got to rely on dependable instruments that can be used all the time with our children. I hope these essential 7 Ms we've been learning will become our magnetic compass that we can always rely upon as dads.

Air Traffic Control

As a pilot, I knew the importance of the air traffic controllers. But it wasn't until many years after I got my pilot's license that I actually stepped foot into an air traffic control tower. I don't know if they allow it anymore, but I called Tampa International Airport and arranged for my son Marky and me to check it out.

It was amazing to witness how much control these guys have over everything the pilots do. When a pilot is in the airport's airspace, he must do everything at the command of the traffic controller. On takeoff, the tower instructs, "November one two three Alpha Bravo, winds two eight zero at eleven, cleared for takeoff on runway two-niner." The tower is communicating with the pilot by the tail number of his aircraft and letting him know that the winds are out of 280 degrees and blowing at 11 knots, and that the pilot is cleared to take off on runway twenty nine. Minutes later: "November one two three Alpha Bravo, turn right heading zero six zero and maintain five thousand, slow to two two zero knots." The tower is vectoring the pilot safely through traffic in the airspace in saying to turn right to a heading of

60 degrees, stay at 5,000 feet in altitude, and slow down to 220 knots.

As a pilot's life is in the hands of the air traffic controller, ours, whether we acknowledge it or not, is in the hands of Someone too. We must have full faith in the one who controls our lives, our Master. We'll get to talk more about our Master in chapter 8.

It was a very stormy summer afternoon in Florida. Even so, my family boarded the seven-passenger plane that was to take us to a friend's house in the Bahamas. The airline was called Vintage Air. The name of the airline should have been my first hint that this was not such a good idea. Visibility was marginal. As a result, we had to deplane and board again several times before we received clearance to take off. After a bumpy takeoff, we soon left behind the Florida coast and were over the Atlantic Ocean.

Suddenly, fire broke out in the right engine, the plane dropped, and we were going down. At that very moment, I looked at my wife and the panicked faces of my children and started thinking about what's most important. I thanked God for what He had done in my life. I thanked Him for my wife, my kids, my family, and what a blessing they've been to me. And, of course, I asked Him to spare us. The elder and very experienced pilot followed protocol and shut down the engine that was burning. He then immediately stabilized the aircraft with just one operable engine. Just as I rely on my Master, the one in the control tower of my life, the pilot contacted the control tower and relied on the controller to vector us back to the airport for an emergency landing. Fortunately, the fire trucks and ambulance on the runway did not have to be dispatched as the pilot brought us in for a rough but safe landing.

Without the proficient pilot and air traffic controller, we may not have made it. As we'll learn in the chapter on knowing your Master, having a clear understanding of who or what controls your life is a life or death matter.

Preflight Inspection

A critical responsibility of a pilot is to do a preflight inspection before he and his passengers board the vessel. He should check out the inside of the aircraft to make sure that all the instruments are working and inspect the outside of the plane, especially its integrity, to ensure that there are no cracks in the wings or fuselage. Even a minor breach can spell disaster once the plane is in the air. Likewise, a father must ensure that he is living a life of integrity as he carries his children on the journey. To compromise, even in the slightest, could be devastating for a child.

As you learned in the chapter on Motive, dark secrets in your life can cause a dangerous breach in your fatherhood fuselage and keep you from growing as a leader in your home. Addictions—sexual, pornographic, gambling, drugs, alcohol—are primary culprits that will keep you from being the dad you want to be.

But addictions are not the only things that deflate. Anything that controls or that has dominion over your mind and heart can do the same thing and needs to be dealt with promptly. A man's integrity, or lack of it, is revealed by what he does when no one else is looking. It is also revealed when others, like your children, are looking. When you get too much change back at the grocery store, what do you do? When you order water at a fast-food restaurant for your kids, do you tell them it's okay to get a Coke out of the self-serve machine? Do you fib about your child's age to get cheaper movie tickets? Modeling integrity to our children is always important, in big things and small. Integrity is crucial for the model father.

Takeoff and Flight

As we take flight as fathers, we need to remember that to be a great prototype for our kids to follow, we must be models not only of integrity but also of humility and courage. In his book *Good to Great*, author Jim Collins wrote that a superb leader "blends extreme personal humility with intense professional will." He or she displays a "fierce resolve" to make the company great.[8] In the same way, to be a superb leader at home, a man needs to show extreme personal humility and intense personal will or courage to do whatever he needs to do to be the best father he can be.

Let's start with humility. Many people think that humility has mostly to do with how you think about yourself. It doesn't. You're not going to be more humble by focusing on yourself.

Humility has more to do with how you think of others. Humility doesn't mean that we think less of ourselves; it just means that we think about ourselves less and others more. Furthermore, humility doesn't mean you have nothing to offer. It means you know exactly what you have to offer, and no more. In his book *Traveling Light*, author Max Lucado gives three tips on cultivating humility. First, assess yourself honestly. Don't cherish exaggerated ideas of your importance. Second, don't take "success" too seriously. If you do, your downfall may be just around the corner. Third, celebrate the significance of others, because they helped you achieve your success in the first place.[9]

Whether it's on the stage before thousands or in the home with his wife and kids, Michael W. Smith says he always strives to have a "posture of humility." "It's about putting others before yourself. It's about serving your family and, if it came down to it, dying for your wife and kids."[10]

And Tony Dungy, a man of great humility himself, shared with me that "being a humble parent means you put your children's interests first. When kids see that, they're going to be drawn to you as a parent and will follow your lead. You may not have anything else to give them, but if you show that humility, that you really care about them, that's going to make an impact far more than a parent who just gives them all kinds of material things."[11]

Do your children keep you humble? Mine do. I was dropping my daughter Emily off at school and then going to speak to a group of men about being better dads. On the way, my daughter said, "Dad, why do you teach men to be better fathers when you haven't mastered it yet?" That hurt, but it was a good question that I wanted to answer. So I said, "I want to share with the men the mistakes I've made and the things I've learned as a father over the years."

Having a "posture of humility," as Michael W. Smith said, is at the very core of any thriving relationship, including your relationship with your child. Why? Simply put, if selfishness is not the opposite of humility, it's pretty close. Selfishness destroys relationships. Humility develops relationships.

Admitting when you're wrong and apologizing to your children is one way to model humility. I've had to ask my kids for forgiveness on many occasions. One time, I was watching an action thriller with my young teenage son. It was kind of scary and had a few off-color words. I was so glued to the flick that I didn't even think how it would affect my son. Emily, my daughter who rules my conscience, walked in the door, took one look at the television, and said, "Uh, Dad, do you really think you should be watching this?" Well, the answer was obvious. I turned off the movie, apologized to my son for not showing more leadership, and found a more productive activity to do with my son. I'm still learning how to be a better parent, and my kids are doing a great job helping me.

A close companion to humility is empathy. Empathy is defined as "the action of understanding, being aware of, being sensitive to, and vicariously experiencing the feelings, thoughts, and experience of another." Empathy is so important in love and leadership. The vast majority of issues in relationships would be resolved if we accurately saw issues from others' perspectives, if we looked at the issues through their lens.

As we were sitting in his office at the Indianapolis Colts facility, well-read coach Jim Caldwell mentioned to me that there are two important components of leadership. The first one didn't surprise me. Jim said it is expertise. The second did. He said it is empathy. "You must have empathy in both parenting and coaching. Whether it's one of my players or one of my children, as a leader, I have to be able to put myself in their shoes. Being a coach has made me a better parent and being a parent made me a better coach. Having kids taught me how to empathize with others."[12]

Empathy involves both the head and the heart. Here are the three As of empathy that a father can use as a guide in loving his children well:

Aware—Be aware of what your child is feeling and
 what's behind that feeling.
Agenda—Set aside your own agenda and focus on
 the needs of your child.
Action—Take action on meeting the needs of
 your child.

In addition to integrity, humility, and empathy, to be a superb leader in the home, a father must also model courage.

Know that your flight will not always be smooth. Every pilot will encounter turbulence, and perhaps even an emergency, while in flight. To be a hero to his kids, an All Pro Dad must have unwavering courage to navigate through those turbulent times in his marriage and in raising his children.

Tony Dungy knows what courage is all about. "Courage is the ability to do the right thing, all the time, no matter how painful or uncomfortable it might be," Tony said to me in his convincing way. "It takes courage to discipline at the right time and in the right way. It takes courage to say no. It takes courage to go against the grain and say, 'You know what, I know everybody else allows their kids to watch these television programs, or dress like that, but I'm not going to allow it.' It takes courage to stand up for your convictions."[13]

And courage means you won't turn back when the storms hit your marriage, even if your emotional fuel tank is depleted. Instead, you will keep your eyes on the compass that points you to these seven truths about marriage that a model husband always keeps on board his life:

Truth #1: Marriage is not just about two people; it's about two people becoming one flesh.

Truth #2: Marriage is not just "for better"; it's also "for worse."

Truth #3: Marriage is not always a stroll in the park; it's a frontline battle in the world.

Truth #4: Marriage is not a fifty-fifty partnership; it's a 100 percent–100 percent give-it-all-you've-got relationship.

Truth #5: Marriage is not just about happiness; it's about holiness.

Truth #6: Marriage is not about getting from your spouse; it's about giving to your spouse.

Truth #7: Marriage is not a quick sprint; it's a lifetime marathon.

Having shared these seven truths with you, I must emphasize again that, if you are married, the very best thing you can do for your children is to love their mother. Love her courageously.

Courage also means that you won't eject from the pilot's seat when you have an unruly passenger in your child, and that you will continue to keep your eye on the compass that points you to these twelve truths about parenting:

Truth #1: Parenting is "heart work." It's not just about outward obedience; it's about the inward attitude of your child.

Truth #2: Parenting requires prayer, patience, and perseverance.

Truth #3: Parenting = relationship + rules.

Relationship – rules = rebellion.

Rules – relationship = rebellion.

Truth #4: Parenting is loving your child by disciplining your child when the rules are broken.

Truth #5: Parenting is sacrificially loving your child—doing what's best for your child no matter what it costs you personally.

Truth #6: Parenting is understanding your child by being a student of your child.

Truth #7: Parenting is unconditionally loving your child for who they are, not for what they do.

Truth #8: Parenting requires speaking absolute truth into your child's life.

Truth #9: Parenting is understanding that the world does not revolve around your child.

Truth #10: Parenting is about failing, forgiving, and asking for forgiveness.

Truth #11: Parenting is being a parent, not a pal.

Truth #12: Parenting is putting your relationship with God first.

No matter what you do for a living, there's one job that all parents share—being a role model for their children. When a father demonstrates consistency in all areas of life and exhibits integrity, humility, empathy, and courage, he's essentially saying to his children, "I love you so much that I'm going to do my absolute best to show you how to do life the right way." When he does so, his children will notice that deep love he has for them. As a result, their respect for their dad will increase and his leadership capacity will continue to grow.

HUDDLE UP AND ASK YOUR CHILD:

1 Do you think I act the same way no matter who I'm with?

2 Do you think I try to do what is right even when it is not best for me?

3 Have you ever seen me do something that wasn't right? What should I have done differently?

4 When I am wrong about something, do I apologize?

5 Who is the best role model you know? Why do you think so highly of him or her?

7

KNOW YOUR MESSAGE

What Do I Need to Share with Others?

Everyone can be great, because
everyone can serve.
—Dr. Martin Luther King Jr.

S houting for her team and jumping with enthusiasm, seventeen-year-old Susan, a cheerleader, was cheering her high school football team in Hollywood, Florida, on to victory. During the third quarter of the game, after a series of emotionally charged plays, Susan realized her heart was pounding abnormally hard even when she wasn't cheering. Something was definitely not right. So she sat out the fourth quarter and then went directly to the emergency room rather than going out to celebrate the big district football victory.

In the ER, tests showed her heart was racing at a pace of 220 beats per minute and had been at that rate for more than two hours. Steps were taken to slow her heart down to a normal rate, but the result was not good. Her heart flatlined. That is, it showed no activity on the heart monitor. In a matter of seconds, Susan heard the call for "Code Blue," which means the patient was under cardiac arrest and required immediate resuscitation. As the doctor and nurses rushed to her side with a defibrillator, she thought about her family. She felt a tube go down her throat, and her eyes closed. She then had an encounter with God that she will never forget and that would change her life forever. The doctors were able to bring Susan back to life. Two days later Susan received her first pacemaker.

God performed a miracle, giving my wife, Susan, a new life, a new heart, and a desire to pursue life with a sense of urgency and purpose—God's purpose. Now, a dozen surgeries and three pacemakers later, Susan continues to live her life with purpose, encourages our kids to live with purpose, and helps other moms do the same through our Family First motherhood program—iMOM. Susan turned her pain into passion, a passion to live purposefully for God. That's her message.

EVERYONE HAS PAIN

Sometimes you wouldn't know it, but everyone has pain. When you meet with your colleague at work, when you catch up with that acquaintance over lunch, or when you talk to another dad at the Little League field, you often hear about how they just made a ton of money from a lucrative investment and are taking the whole family to Italy, how awesome their marriage is, or how their child just made the All-Star team, the honor roll, and the incoming freshman class at a prestigious college.

I know when I hear those stories, even while I'm listening, my mind often retreats, I climb into my mental foxhole, the surrender flag goes up, and I feel a sense of defeat. I ask myself, "What did I do wrong?" My interrogation of myself continues. "Why isn't my child on the starting team?" "Why isn't my marriage more like his?" Well, more often than not, things are not as they appear.

David and Kristina were friends of ours. We enjoyed dinner, events, and other things together with them and their children. I confess, Susan and I were always somewhat jealous of their awesome relationship as a couple. They were sweeter than honey to each other, and kind words to one another always flowed from their lips. We wanted more of what they had. On more than one occasion, Susan would pull me aside and ask, "Why can't we be more like David and Kristina?" "I know," I responded with a twinge of longing for what they had too, "they've got a great marriage."

Several years later they were separated and went through a terrible divorce. The relational cancer that they knew about, but had been hiding since the beginning of their marriage, had metastasized and spread to the vital organs of their relationship. Bitterness, anger, secrets, and distrust were all a part of it. Their marriage died a slow death. It may be severe, it may be minimal, but everyone has pain.

Some people, for various reasons, aren't comfortable or secure enough in their own skin to be real about the pain in their life. Am I suggesting, as some do, that you should just dump your garbage on the table with every person you come in contact with? Of course not. Some things between a husband

and wife, a father and child, should remain confidential. And when they are shared with others, permission should usually be obtained first so as not to breach a trust in your relationship. What I am suggesting is that authenticity and vulnerability in relationships matter. Your scars can be used for good. It can be your message of hope to others. Your pain, handled rightly, can turn into your passion and your message to the world.

WHAT WILL I DO WITH PAIN?

We already established that everyone has suffering and trials at some point in his or her life, some more than others. So the question is not whether you and I will suffer. The question you need to ask yourself is: "What will I do with pain?"

From the time we are born, our natural trajectory, or path, is to live a life pointed at ourselves. A baby does not come out of the womb thinking, *I'm going to sleep through the night so Mom and Dad can get some rest.* And have you ever heard a toddler say, "I really don't want that brand-new toy. Let's save the money and give it to some people who really need it"? Or, what about that teenager? Do you think you'll hear, "Dad, I cannot believe how hard you work for our family. Why don't you take it easy while I get some chores done?" Of course not. The point is, unless someone or something intervenes to change that path that focuses on self, it will continue to be our trajectory for the rest of our lives.

That's where pain comes in. Pain can do one of two things. It can turn our trajectory even more inward on ourselves, or it can impact our trajectory and turn it outward toward others. If we allow it, the pain we experience can be that intervening force to get the focus off of what we want for ourselves and onto the needs of others.

My guess is you've met people who have become very bitter, angry, and ever more self-focused as a result of being wounded by a family member, having gone through the pain of divorce, or having suffered through the loss of a job. On the other hand, you've probably met people who have been injected with that kind of pain but have been willing to allow it to change the course of their life to one that is more others-centered.

Think of pain as a relational bonding agent. Pain allows you to identify with another person who is going through the same thing and for them to identify with you. You share something in common that binds you together.

Pain also allows you to empathize with the other person. As we learned in the previous chapter on being a good role model, empathy is an important character trait of a loving leader. As you empathize with others, you experience similar feelings, thoughts, and emotions and then take action based on what you've experienced to meet the needs of others. As a result, others are aware that you know what they are going through, and, therefore, will listen to what you have to say. Think about it. Who can better help a parent of a Down syndrome child than a parent of a Down syndrome child? Who can better help someone who is going through a divorce than someone who went through a divorce?

Tony and Lauren Dungy have a son, Jordan, who was born with a rare condition called congenital insensitivity to pain. He is not able to feel pain. Because Jordan cannot feel pain, he's burned his hand on the stove without realizing it. He's also broken his leg after jumping off the couch. He's gone through countless surgeries, been in several casts, and had multiple wheelchairs. In fact, as I write these words this morning, Jordan has had surgery on yet another broken bone.

Jordan's inability to feel pain in his body made me realize that pain is important in the sense that it protects us from harming ourselves physically. Yet, at the same time, not feeling pain physically has ironically caused Jordan to experience pain emotionally. He has not been able to do all the things that other kids get to do and develop all the friendships he'd like. That emotional pain that Jordan, as well as Tony and Lauren, has felt, prompted Tony and Lauren to speak out about the importance of kids being sensitive to special-needs children and being good friends to others, especially those, like Jordan, who are going through difficulty. They've also written a children's book about it called *You Can Be a Friend*. Tony and Lauren have allowed the emotional pain Jordan experiences to be a relational agent and an intervening force for good. They've turned that pain into a passion to help others. That's their message.

In his book *The Problem of Pain*, C. S. Lewis pointed out that pain is a megaphone designed to wake us up. If we will be taught by our pain, we can be an unstoppable force for good in the world. Don't run from it. Make it serve you and others.

Everyone Has a Message

Everyone has a message. You do too. In a moment, I'll share how your message can be born out of either pleasure or pain. Maybe you've discovered your message; maybe you haven't. Your message is an integral part of your life story. It's something you have to say to the world. Ultimately, your message should be something of eternal value that you have to share with others because of your love for them, not because you get anything in return.

But when you pour that love into others' lives, you'll benefit too. You'll find that you're not alone in your suffering. People will, more often than not, come out of the woodwork and share a similar story of pain with you. Also, as your message meets a need or lightens the grief in someone else's life, you will experience a deep sense of satisfaction and joy that no amount of money can buy. Playwright George Bernard Shaw once said, "This is the true joy of life: the being used up for a purpose recognized by yourself as a mighty one; being a force of nature instead of a feverish, selfish little clot of ailments and grievances, complaining that the world will not devote itself to making you happy."[1]

Everyone's Message Must Matter

I want to caution you. Should you just pursue, with all your might, whatever you're most passionate about in your life just because you want to share it with the world? No. Your message should align with your mission to love and should flow from a pure motive. Your message must matter.

For just a moment, let's look into the future. Your life on earth is coming to an end. You look back on all the things you have done, good and bad, right and wrong. You smile at the joys you've experienced; you weep at the pain you've gone through. You think back on what your life has meant. Do you see a life that you lived for yourself, a shallow and hollow life? Or do you see a life that mattered, where you gave of your time, talent, and treasure to others? You can only have a life with meaning if you give it away. Your message helps you do that.

A Message Born out of Pleasure or Pain?

Do you know your message? Sometimes, what gives you pleasure in your life may be what you're passionate about. It may be your message to share with others. Eric Liddell, often called the "Flying Scotsman" because of his speed, was a Scottish athlete who won a gold medal in the 1924 Summer Olympics in Paris. The classic movie *Chariots of Fire* was about Liddell's amazing life of sports and faith. In the movie, Liddell said, "I believe God made me for a purpose, but He also made me fast. And when I run I feel His pleasure."[2] Being a runner gave Eric Liddell a great deal of pleasure not because it made him feel good, but because he felt the pleasure of God as he used his platform as an Olympic runner to share his convictions and his faith. He turned his pleasure into his passion, and his passion into a desire to reach out and love others. That was his message.

But, as we discussed previously, more often than not, what causes you pain in your life is the force that changes your life trajectory toward loving people. However, that trajectory doesn't always change right away. Pain sometimes comes into our lives and partially paralyzes us at first, physically or emotionally. We may suffer physically for a while, like Susan did after her cardiac arrest. Or, we may suffer emotionally from things like broken relationships or depression. Our natural tendency is to fight that temporary paralysis like an enemy; but instead, we should welcome it as a friend. It can be a good thing. It forces us to pause and ponder what's really important in this world. It's part of the process to get us ready for good works. As we pause and ponder from our paralysis, we should ask God to show us our message and to turn our pain into our passion, and our passion into a love for others.

My Message

My dad and I love each other. He's an incredibly talented man. I actually think he could have been the president of the United States. People love him. He's a deep thinker. He and I had many deep and philosophical conversations as I was growing up. He's given me a love for the outdoors. We've gone on quite a few hunting and fishing trips over the years. He's taught me to persevere. He's taught me the importance of family and relationships. We have a wonderful relationship and have spent some wonderful times together.

But we've experienced heartache together as well. Ever since I can remember, he's been an alcoholic. His father was too. As a teen, I remember lying in my bed late in the night, tears welling up in my eyes, not knowing if my dad was going to make it home. *Where is he?* I worried and wondered. *Is he okay? Did he die in a car accident? Did someone else get hurt too?* Fear gripped my heart and paralyzed my mind. Then, during the day, there were always questions. *Is he drinking today? Can I bring friends home or not? Should I believe him when he promises not to drink anymore?* And anyone who has a family member or friend who's an alcoholic or drug abuser knows that one of the biggest things associated with it are a lot of lies and deception and a resulting distrust in the relationship.

It has caused pain in his life. It has also caused pain in my life. But I've used it to help others. I now have a great passion to speak truth into people's lives. Not only truth about alcoholism, but truth about relationships, truth about marriage, and truth about fatherhood. I've turned that pain into a passion. That's my message.

TRUETT'S MESSAGE

As Truett Cathy and I continued to visit at Chick-fil-A head-quarters in Atlanta, Georgia, he talked more about his nonexistent relationship with his father. "I didn't want to grow up being like my dad," Truett shared in a solemn tone, still seeming to feel the father wound from decades past. "He was the last one you would go to for advice or counseling. I never heard him say, 'Thank you.' I never heard him say that he loved me, and he never kissed me. He argued with my mom all the time."[3]

Truett determined from the beginning to be different as a man, husband, and father. He has been a devoted husband of sixty-three years to his childhood sweetheart, Jeannette. He has been a loving father to his three children, Dan, Bubba, and Trudy; a caring grandfather to his twelve grandchildren; and a doting great-grandfather to his eleven great-grandchildren. Truett was also determined to do his best to ensure that other children did not grow up with his pain. So he established WinShape foster care homes where loving families take care of children who don't have parents to look to. Truett has been a father figure to thousands. And now, Truett works with our

Family First fatherhood program, All Pro Dad, to get fathers more actively involved in their children's lives. That's his message.

ABE'S MESSAGE

After learning that one of his former football players was in jail for an alleged murder, Blake High School head football coach Abe Brown went to visit this young man. Painfully convicted that he had taught young men how to play football but neglected to teach them enough about how to live life, Abe Brown's life trajectory changed drastically. He moved from teacher and coach to full-time work in Florida prisons. He dedicated his life, inside and outside prison walls, to being a coach and father figure to young men. I was privileged to serve with Abe, before his passing from this life, on his board of directors at Abe Brown Ministries in Tampa, Florida. It was an honor to watch this man demonstrate his love and leadership to so many fatherless prisoners. That was Abe's message.

NATHANIEL'S MESSAGE

Nathaniel Timothy Kuck was born prematurely on June 6, 1997, with multiple birth anomalies. He was said to have an undiagnosed syndrome. Surgeries, therapies, sickness, and hospital visits all became a normal part of his life. After proving himself to be "a miracle boy," beating the odds time and again by overcoming many physical obstacles and challenges, on November 13, 2001, at an early age of four and a half, Nathaniel joined God.

That sorrow of losing their precious child gave Nathaniel's parents, Tim and Marie Kuck, whose family also owns Regal Boats international boat company, their message—Nathaniel's Hope, an organization dedicated to sharing hope with kids with special needs and their families. In addition to its other services, Nathaniel's Hope partners with churches around the country to provide free respite care to families with special-needs children. The pain Tim and Marie experienced impacted the trajectory of their lives in an indescribable way. But even as hard as it was, they allowed pain to be their teacher. It gave them a passion to serve thousands of other families with special-needs children. That's their message.

YOUR MESSAGE

Maybe you could relate to my story, or perhaps Truett's, Abe's, or Tim and Marie's stories in some way. Maybe you couldn't. But either way, there is one thing I know: you've got a story. Maybe you've discovered it, maybe you haven't. Maybe it's a story overflowing with pleasure, or it may be a story filled with pain. So, what's your message?

Perhaps your message was, or will be, born out of pleasure. Maybe you get pleasure as a schoolteacher helping children to learn. Coaching kids may be the path you really enjoy. Maybe volunteering your time to mentor a fatherless child or serving hungry folks at food shelters brings you joy because you know you're giving them something to help alleviate their pain. Or, perhaps it's regularly serving the widow next door financially or by helping her with the upkeep of her home.

Maybe your message was, or in the future will be, conceived in pain. You've experienced the pain of prostate or breast cancer, losing a job, financial problems, divorce, or alcoholism. You're going through or just went through a harsh winter season in your life, full of dreary emotional skies and a brown landscape for your family. But, as I mentioned earlier, that winter season is extremely important and shouldn't just be tolerated. It should be embraced. If the trees didn't drop their leaves, the flowers didn't wilt, and the grass didn't die, we wouldn't have such rich foliage and vibrant growth in the spring. That dreadful season of your life that you wanted to put behind you is exactly what you should put in front of others and share with them, for your growth and theirs. Whatever it is, it can be used for good. Turn your pain into passion. And your passion into your message to love others.

Okay, if you're still stuck in a rut and have no idea what your message is or can be, think about how you can use your time, your talent, your treasure, or all three, to serve people in need on a consistent basis. You may be able to invest some of your time with a young man who didn't have a dad growing up. You may be really skilled with numbers and can use your gift to help a single mom develop a budget. Think about your areas of giftedness that we discussed in the Makeup chapter and use those gifts. And most of us have the ability to give some of the treasure that we've been given to people who need it. And remember, it doesn't have to be tax deductible.

Simply showing kindness to others can pull you out of the rut as well. Remember the four things we need to do to show kindness that we talked about in the chapter on Mind-set? First, see needs of people all around us. Second, sympathize with people's pain and struggles. Third, seize the moment. Fourth, spend lavishly to meet the need. As you show kindness to others, you will hopefully experience the pleasure of helping others, which in turn could very well develop into your passion and a way to give of yourself to others. As you develop your passion, just remember: your message is not a one-and-done kind of thing. Your message is about lasting change in your life and the lives of those you touch. Lasting change takes lasting commitment.

Author, educator, and civil rights leader Howard Thurman once said, "Don't ask yourself what the world needs, ask yourself what makes you come alive and then go do that because that's what the world needs, people who have come alive."[4] Things that give us pleasure and things that give us pain both prod us to come alive. They give us passion to do something significant in our lives for someone else.

Hopefully, you now know your message or know how to develop your message. So, why is knowing your message important as a father? First, when you know your message and share it with others, you're demonstrating to your children that life is bigger than just you. You have something significant to share that is beyond yourself. And by doing so, you're demonstrating your love for others. Second, you're teaching your children that life is bigger than them too. The universe, whether they know it or not, does not revolve around them. And it's our responsibility to show them how to alter their inborn, selfish trajectory. Loving others is our great and eternal duty. So, after you've developed your message, help your kids develop theirs. Let me give you some practical ways to do so.

Your Child's Message

"Wow!" my son said as he tried on my reading glasses. "I can see really good up close, but far away—it's blurry." That made me think. All children, whether they need glasses or not, are "near-sighted." Like my son, they only see what's up close, what's happening today at school or tonight after dinner. Stuff in the distance is more fuzzy and out of focus. I can assure you, most of our children are not thinking about the long-term significance of developing their message, of serving and giving to others. They're much more focused on themselves, just as you and I were at their age.

And our children, more often than not, have not experienced the pleasure or pain that we have had in our lives and, therefore, may not know their message yet. Parents are usually more "far-sighted," and it's our job to help our kids see things in the distance, what's in their future. As fathers, we need to help them start developing a far-sighted vision for loving others.

There are at least three ways to get your kids started in the process of developing their message. The first and easiest thing you can do is to include them as you pursue your message. Whether you develop your message through your time, talent, or treasure, be sure to involve your children as much as possible. Take them with you. Talk to them about why you're doing what you're doing. Explain to them that we are just trustees of our time, talent, and treasure and we have a fiduciary duty to be good stewards of those things.

The second thing you can do is to participate with your children in various service projects. Sometimes that's easier said than done with our kids since they're often focused, as we are, on their own wants and desires. I've also found that some food shelters don't allow children under sixteen to volunteer. And when I wanted to take my kids on a local missions trip to a prison, I learned that they have to be at least eighteen years old. But we can't use those excuses to keep our kids from serving. There are more opportunities out there than we can tackle.

I found an easy thing we could do with our kids, and we didn't even have to leave the house to do it. After Susan and

I had returned from the grocery store, with a little coercion, we got our teens together in our kitchen. We assembled some "manna," or food bags for the homeless and hungry. We filled large Ziploc bags with nonperishable items like granola bars, beef jerky, peanuts, fruit cups, and vegetable juice. Now, when we're out in the car and see someone in need on the median or street corner, we just give them a manna bag. It's a simple gesture that didn't cost much or take too much time, but maybe this small act of kindness not only will help the recipients but also will help our children develop a vision for their message.

The third thing you can do to help your children develop their message is to be observant. Keep your eyes open and see if you notice something tugging at their hearts and then work with them to pursue it.

As we pulled out of Kanakuk Kamp parking lot in Branson, Missouri, a few summers ago, Susan noticed tears welling up in the eyes of our then–fourteen-year-old son Marky. A couple of days before that, we went to a sister camp of Kanakuk for inner-city youth, Kids Across America, where we volunteered for the day. Having played basketball and football with a number of boys from Tampa's inner city, Marky had started to develop a desire to help those kids in need who didn't have all the things that we have.

That experience seemed to further that interest. So the following year, he raised the funds, with a little help from us, to bring forty boys from Tampa's urban community on a lengthy bus ride to Kids Across America. I, along with several others, joined as a chaperone, and Marky volunteered at the camp and worked for the week. Serving young men in need may or may not ultimately be a passion for my son; that's not my call. Directing him toward his life message is, whatever that may be.

Dr. Martin Luther King Jr. told us what greatness is all about when he said, "Everyone can be great because everyone can serve."[5] When you have a vision for your message to serve others and passionately set your sights on that message for the long haul, your capacity to love will greatly expand. And as you start seeing with clarity how you can love and lead others with your message, you can then work with your children and start the process of helping them develop their message.

HUDDLE UP AND ASK YOUR CHILD:

1. What is the most painful thing that has ever happened to you? What did you learn from it?

2. What is one time you really enjoyed helping someone else?

3. Who do you think really needs our help? What should we do for them? Why should we do it?

KNOW YOUR MASTER

Who or What Am I Living For?

All men seek happiness. This is without exception. Whatever different means they employ, they all tend to this end ... This is the motive of every action of every man.

—Blaise Pascal

What drives the decisions you make? It's pretty simple actually. Philosopher and mathematician Blaise Pascal touched on it a few hundred years ago. Everything you do, everything, is driven by what you *think* will maximize your happiness.

Let me illustrate. Why are you reading this book? Because you think it will help you become a better father and, in turn, have a happier family, thus making you happier. Or maybe you are reading it because your wife handed it to you and you think reading it will make her happy, and if she's happy with you, you'll be happier. So, if you accept the premise that happiness is what drives you, it is well worth a moment to look at two important things about this word, *happiness*.

First, just because you are living for happiness doesn't necessarily make you a selfish person. It depends on if your happiness is derived from the right source. The problem is that oftentimes what we think will maximize our happiness is deeply flawed. We often misunderstand what makes us truly happy. Second, as I'm using the word *happy* in this book, I'm not referring to a superficial, flimsy feeling based on mere circumstance or happenstance as many use the word today, but rather a true, deep, firm, lasting joy and contentment.

So what does a discussion about what gives us this ultimate happiness have to do with being an All Pro Dad and the fatherhood fundamentals of love and leadership? Everything. Just as the earth revolves around the sun and keeps a constant orbit as a result of the gravitational pull of the sun, our life will revolve around what we depend on for our happiness. The gravitational pull of the source of our happiness will be so strong that it will influence everything else we do, including what kind of father we'll be. We will live our lives for who or what we think gives us ultimate happiness—our master. That doesn't mean we will be only focused on things that make us happy, but that our main focus—the primary recipient of our thoughts, affections, attention, and energy—will be on what we look to for our happiness.

Who or What Are You Living For?

Everything we have discussed in this book about how to be an All Pro Dad hangs on how you answer this one question: Who or what are you living for? If you miss this, you miss everything. If you don't get this right, you won't be the dad your kids need you to be. So as we ascend higher and approach the summit we are striving for as dads, let's do some serious soul-searching and spend some time on the climb to answer this critical question.

Whether you know it or not, you have a master. Someone or something rules your life. It's where you place your affections and attention. It's your hope for happiness. Not sure who or what you're living for? Want to find out?

Let me ask you a few questions: What's the first thing you think about when you wake up in the morning? What's the last thing you think about when you go to bed at night? What wakes you up at night? What consumes your thoughts? What consumes your time? What consumes your money? If you put all those answers together, you may find out who or what you serve, what rules your life—who your master is. I'm not suggesting that if your mind is focused on your job, or lack of one, or on financial matters for a season, that work or money is your master. Likewise, if basking in the joys of your marriage or experiencing challenges with your children are occupying your waking hours, that doesn't mean you are serving the wrong master. It all comes down to determining who or what your life revolves around.

If your happiness comes from fame, fortune, power, or pleasure, then your life will be all about you; and if you're always focused on you, then you won't be focused on others. Loving others, even your spouse and children, won't be a priority for you, even though you say your family comes first.

If fame rules your life, then your adrenaline will pump when accolades, awards, and applause come your way. You'll roll out the welcome mat for as much recognition as you can get. Whatever you can do to get your name on the building or in the program, you'll do, since you think that is what will make you happy. Or maybe fortune revs your engine. Amassing wealth to store in vaults and banks in the name of "financial security" is something many do. Reckless spending on things also often accompanies money. Using money for lavish comfort is something you may be doing. Pursuing power may be your master. You'll do just about anything for a title that makes you feel superior or a position where you can wield authority over others. Maybe pleasure seeking is at the top of your list. Recreation and sports may command your time and treasure. You may be a slave to sexual satisfaction outside of marriage or to pornography. Perhaps it's the bottle or prescription drugs that you're worshipping.

Now, fame, fortune, power, and pleasure are not all inherently evil. For example, money can be used for noble purposes to help those in need of a good, hot meal, or to assist an elderly neighbor who can't pay the electric bill. Positions of authority can be used to make corporate decisions that serve others inside and outside the workplace. And pleasure in its proper place and with the appropriate people can be downright fun!

I Want to Control

Much of what I'm talking about here has to do with control. Fame, fortune, power, and pleasure all have an element of control. We want to control our spouse's temper, our teen's behavior, our baby's safety, our in-laws' manipulation, our staff's work ethic, and our friend's loyalty. We want to control conception, births, aging, health, and even death.

Business consultant Barry Banther has been a very close friend for over two decades and my go-to guy for wisdom, advice, and encouragement. During a visit in my office, I shared with Barry my recent struggles. I threw out to him all the things I've been thinking about lately—my fears, my frustrations, my doubts—relating to my family, faith, work, and future. Barry is one of those guys who can slice through the clutter and cut to the chase quickly. After he patiently listened to and empathized with me, he said, "Mark, many of your struggles boil down to the issue of control." He shared with me that "as we get older, we come to the startling realization that we are not in control of most things in life and never were. We just thought we were."[1]

There have always been many things that attract me to Susan. But somehow, in the early years of our marriage, I thought I had the power to control and change the things I didn't like. Of course, I learned quickly the error of my thinking. And when our children were younger, Susan and I pretty much controlled what they ate, what they wore, what they watched, where they went, and who they went with. But in reality, even at those young ages, there still was so much that was out of our control. For example, even if they had their bicycle helmet on and we did our best to teach them safety, protecting them from getting hit by a car was not completely within our control. Of course, now that they are much older, all in their teens and twenties, things are much different. We control even less.

It's amazing to me that many of the executives and celebrities I've interviewed, who seem to be in complete control of everything they do, realize how little they really do control in their lives. Jude Thompson, former CEO of Papa Johns, summarized what I'm saying well. Jude shared with me, "If you think you rule and control your own life, that's fool's gold."[2] And Dave Dunkel, CEO of KForce professional staffing, agrees. "We need to understand that we don't control our lives and need to make the choice to deny self and follow the One who does."[3]

Mark Richt, head football coach for the University of Georgia, knows what he can control and what he cannot. As Mark and I spoke about this, he said with a deep sense of confidence that "every person comes at some time or another to the end of their strength or their wisdom or their sanity, whatever it may be, and then if we only rely on our own strengths and our own abilities, we'll come up really short. There may be moments, seasons in life, where we seem to have it all together and think we are in control, but sooner or later, life's going to drop you to your knees. You have to decide whether or not you're going to look inward or upward. If you look inward, you find emptiness. If you look upward, you find strength beyond anything you can imagine."[4]

Bottom line? There is so little in life that I can control. There's only one person I know whom I even have a shot at controlling—me. And that's not a sure thing. How about when you lost that job? Or when your child was diagnosed with a serious illness? Or when you had that car accident? Or when your father passed away unexpectedly? We need to get real. How much control do we really have? Not as much as we want or hope for, and because of that, we need to direct our hopes to the only one who has control—the Master.

MY SEARCH FOR THE ANSWER

One day when I was a kid, I was playing with some toys in my room, like all little boys do. Suddenly, intruders came into our house and grabbed me. Then I watched them overpower my mom and dad, tie them up, and take them away. It was unbearable. "No, no, please no," I pleaded with their captors. My arm reached for Mom and Dad. "Don't leave me, please don't." My cries did not help. In an instant, they were gone. I was alone, sobbing uncontrollably. Then, I awoke and was safe and secure in my mom's arms. She and Dad had witnessed a horrific dream I was having with my eyes open the entire time. Before you start psychoanalyzing my weird dream, know that this wasn't a symptom of something terrible that occurred in my life. It just happened.

I know this may sound a bit strange to you, but as a young boy, fear of death found its way not only into my dreams on a number of occasions but also into my waking hours. For months I grappled to understand this thing called death. Why were these thoughts entering my mind? I have no idea. I wasn't so much afraid of the act of death, but rather what happens when I die. It was really a fear of the unknown. What will happen to me, my mom, my dad, and my two brothers when we die? Will I see them again? Where am I going when I die? Do I just get buried, with worms eating my decaying body, and that's it? Or is there something more? Is there hope for true, eternal happiness?

Last time I checked, ten out of ten people die. Death is certain. But people don't want to talk about it. Why? Well, let's face it: we fear it. And besides, it's flat-out uncomfortable and depressing to talk about our eventual demise. So what do we do instead? Author Os Guinness explains: "We are reluctant, even afraid, to admit that we all, without exception, will die. We surround ourselves with entertaining distractions so we don't have to think about death. We tranquilize ourselves with the trivial. Has any generation ever been able to divert itself so happily for so long and with so many fascinating toys as ours? With our Blackberries, iPhones, iPods, and TiVos, we can lose ourselves in virtual reality and be entertained and distracted forever—'amusing ourselves to death,' as bestselling author Neil Postman puts it."[5]

I needed answers to these and other ultimate questions, such as: Where did I come from? Did I "just happen"? Was I created? As a boy I answered those questions when I realized who my Master is. But I still needed to substantiate what I believed deep down inside and knew in my heart to be true. So my search for evidence began during my teen years, kept going through college, and continues today.

I Want Evidence—Is There a Creator?

As I mentioned earlier, I'm an attorney—actually, a "recovering" attorney. In law school and in the law practice, I studied and learned the importance of analyzing carefully, questioning hypotheses, and establishing evidence to advocate for my side of a case. This analytical and interrogating mentality has been somewhat of a curse in life as I question and doubt a lot, and trust only a little. But the blessing, if there is one, lies in my diving very deep into the facts and evidence. After many years of studying history, archeology, biology, and sociology relating to man's existence, I found clear and convincing evidence that established the case for a Creator.

The First Piece of Evidence

The first piece of evidence is found in the conception of the universe. I could accept that the universe just happened and everyone and everything were randomly formed out of tiny microscopic organisms and particles that somehow came together in a miraculous way. Or I could believe there was a mastermind, a Creator behind the complexities of the universe.

Logically, something cannot just come out of nothing. Whatever begins to exist has a cause. The universe began to exist; therefore the universe had a cause. In other words, everything that has a beginning has a beginner. The universe had a beginning; therefore it had a Beginner. The materialist view, that it just happened, has little authority to support it and takes phenomenal faith to accept it.

Earlier, I introduced you to renowned pediatric neuro-surgeon Dr. Ben Carson. As I interviewed him for this book, I was captivated by his every word as he talked about the complexities of the universe. "I look at the universe. I look at how complex our solar system is, which is just a speck in the universe, and it's so organized that astronomers can predict seventy years hence when a comet is coming. How did that kind of organization come out of nothing?"

Carson continued: "So I tell people who believe that we evolved from a slime pit that 'You don't have any evidence of that and the fact of the matter is, that is your religion because it requires huge leaps of faith to come up with those things.' Even Darwin himself said that his theory would be proved or disproved by the discovery of fossil remains. He said they weren't sophisticated enough to find those fossils yet, but in fifty to a hundred years they would be. Well, that was 150 years ago and we still haven't found them. And why haven't we found them? Because they don't exist. So, that requires a huge amount of faith. More faith, quite frankly, than I have."[6]

The Second Piece of Evidence

The second piece of evidence that establishes the case for a Creator is found in the complexities of the human body. Saint Augustine (AD 354–430), ancient North African theologian and bishop of Hippo, makes us think about our amazing bodies in saying, "Men go abroad to wonder at the heights of mountains, at the huge waves of the sea, at the long courses of the rivers, at the vast compass of the ocean, at the circular motions of the stars, and they pass by themselves without wondering."[7] Have you ever wondered? I have.

Every organ of our body is incredibly complex, works in concert with other parts of our body, and has an important purpose. Take, for example, our brain.

Dr. Carson shared with me the complexities of the human brain, saying, "When I look at the complexity of the human brain, with hundreds of billions of interconnections, I know that it didn't just happen. It remembers everything you've ever seen, everything you've ever heard. It can process more than two million bits of information per second. There is no computer that can even come close to our brains."

Carson added, "If we just happened, based on Darwin's theory of evolution and survival of the fittest, then none of us would care about anybody else. We'd only care about ourselves. There would be no such thing as a person who is loving and self-sacrificing in order to help somebody else. So there's a lot more to our brains than just the neurons and the synapses. There's the intangible product of the brain, which is called a mind and a spirit."[8]

How can anyone really suggest that our brain and the way we think "just happened" by a series of random acts occurring and coming together? The same could be said about the heart, the eyes, and every other part of our being.

The Third Piece of Evidence

The universe itself, including planet Earth, is the third massive exhibit of evidence that establishes the case for a creator. During a recent fly-fishing trip with my brothers, Bill and Bob, to Katmai National Park in Alaska, in addition to catching a lot of fish, I learned about the amazing sockeye and silver salmon. These creatures hatch, grow, then swim downstream into the Pacific Ocean where they spend one to eight years and travel thousands of miles, sometimes as far as an area north of the Hawaiian Islands. After that time, they somehow are able to navigate back to the very Alaskan river where they started. Scientists believe they miraculously do so by either a sense of smell, the earth's magnetic field, an internal GPS, or a combination of these tracking systems.

The salmon then swim many more miles upstream against the current and obstacles, lay their eggs, and die. The life cycle then starts all over again.[9] I still wonder how these animals and so many others do what they do. I wonder how our ecosystem works in wonderful harmony. And I still wonder how the sun, moon, and stars hang effortlessly in the sky.

Did it all happen by chance—by a random series of chemical, physiological, and atmospheric accidents?

The Fourth Piece of Evidence

The fourth piece of evidence that establishes the case for a creator is found in the moral law. While there are different cultures in our world with different customs, laws, and rituals, there are overarching standards of right and wrong. Murder is wrong. Rape is repulsive. Stealing is bad. Truth is right. Peace is desired. Sharing is good. There is a moral law that has been planted in the hearts and minds of every human being. It is a law that tells us what is right and what is wrong. To paraphrase C. S. Lewis, a deep thinker on this subject, we all find ourselves under a moral law we did not make and cannot quite forget even if we try, which we know we ought to obey. As Lewis said, there is a real moral law "which none of us made, but which we find pressing on us."[10]

The Fifth Piece of Evidence

The fifth piece of evidence is found in man's yearning for something more and better in life. Things of this world don't make us ultimately happy, even though we search like crazy for it. "More and better" cannot be found in the created, only in the Creator. Said Lewis, "If I find in myself a desire which no experience in this world can satisfy, the most probable explanation is that I was made for another world."[11]

We were made for more. Has anything in your life ever really brought you long-term satisfaction? In your relentless pursuit of maximizing your happiness, have you really ever found this thing called eternal joy? Things will never ultimately satisfy us; only one Person can. So my studied analysis of all the evidence pointed me to a Creator of the universe and a Creator of mankind.

I Want More Evidence—Who Is the Creator?

If we accept the evidence that there is a Creator, we'll want to ask, "Who then is the Creator?" During my years of studying and analyzing various world religions, I was continually drawn back to the Creator—the God of the Old and New Testaments of the Bible. God reveals Himself through creation and His Word—the Bible. But is the Bible reliable? After years of research, I found that the answer is a resounding "Yes!" for several reasons. The Bible is unique in its continuity. Can you imagine any book written over a fifteen-hundred-year span and over forty generations, penned by forty authors, written on three continents and in three languages?[12] And can you imagine that same book telling one continuous, congruent story that is 100 percent accurate and flawless from beginning to end? Only one book in all of human history can make this claim.

The Bible is also unique in its historical manuscript evidence. There are more than twenty-four thousand extant manuscripts, or existing handwritten copies, today. One manuscript fragment dates back to as little as fifty years from the original writings in AD 50–100. And the earliest copy of the complete New Testament is from AD 325, or about 225 years from the date it was written. Next to the New Testament, the greatest amount of manuscript testimony of any ancient book is from Homer's *Iliad*. Fewer than 650 Greek manuscripts of his work exist today. And the span of time from the original writing to the earliest copy on hand is four hundred to five hundred years. Thus, if one discards the Bible as being unreliable, then he must discard all literature of antiquity.[13]

THE VERDICT

If I believe in the authenticity, reliability, and accuracy of the Word of God, then it follows that I must believe that Jesus' claims to be God are true. Otherwise I must dismiss Him as a liar and lunatic. Bono, front man for the rock group U2, puts it this way:

> [Jesus being God] isn't farfetched to me. Look, the secular response to the Christ story always goes like this: he was a great prophet, obviously a very interesting guy, had a lot to say along the lines of other great prophets, be they Elijah, Muhammad, Buddha, or Confucius.

But actually Christ doesn't allow you that. He doesn't let you off that hook. Christ says: *No. I'm not saying I'm a teacher, don't call me teacher. I'm not saying I'm a prophet. I'm saying: "I'm the Messiah." I'm saying: "I am God incarnate." And people say: No, no, please, just be a prophet. A prophet, we can take. . . . But don't mention the "M" word! Because, you know, we're gonna have to crucify you. And he goes . . . actually I am the Messiah.* At this point, everyone starts staring at their shoes, and says: *Oh, my God, he's gonna keep saying this.* So what you're left with is: either Christ was who He said He was—the Messiah—or a complete nutcase. . . . The idea that the entire course of civilization for over half of the globe could have its fate changed and turned upside-down by a nutcase, for me, that's farfetched. . . . But I love the idea of the Sacrificial Lamb. I love the idea that God says: "Look, you cretins, there are certain results to the way we are, to selfishness, and there's a mortality as part of your very sinful nature, and, let's face it, you're not living a very good life, are you? There are consequences to actions." The point of the death of Christ is that Christ took on the sins of the world, so that what we put out did not come back to us, and that our sinful nature does not reap the obvious death. That's the point. It should keep us humbled. . . . It's not our own good works that get us through the gates of Heaven.[14]

Bono, in an unconventional way, makes his point. Either I accept Jesus Christ's claims or I dismiss Him as a liar and lunatic. Either I trust Him or I don't. There is no in between. Trust means I have complete confidence that Jesus is who He says He is—the living Son of the living God. And it also means I have complete confidence that He did what He said He did: He came to earth in human flesh, as a man and yet still God. He took all of my sin that separates me from God upon Himself. He died on the cross carrying that sin. By His death, the verdict is entered—not guilty. I am declared not guilty of my sin, and by His resurrection I am restored to a right relationship with God and will live with Him for eternity in heaven.

I want to make it clear that I don't just trust God with my head and not my heart. I ultimately trust in God not because of the evidence or human reason, but because of God's revelation of Himself to me.

C. S. Lewis said that human history is "the long terrible story of man trying to find something other than God which will make him happy."[15] So maybe it's time for you to rewrite that story and trust God. He's your source of life, true happiness, and love. Author Todd Gongwer said it best in his book *Lead . . . for God's Sake:* "If your life is not built on the foundation of what your Creator created you for first—to glorify Him in your life through your love for Him and for others—you will, I repeat, will ultimately fail to be your best in this life."[16]

THE SOURCE

The Florida aquifer, which underlies the entire state, is an underground body of rock that includes caverns of water that supply nearly 100 percent of the state's drinking water. If Floridians only relied on surface water without the underlying source of the aquifer at our disposal, a drought of mega proportions would soon occur.

In our lives, God is the aquifer of love. God is love and, therefore, the source of love. He is our deep wellspring—our source of continual supply—of love. If God is not your Master, you'll only be able to love others with human love—a surface love that is limited and sometimes polluted with contaminated thinking. But if God is your Master, you'll be able to tap into His deep, unlimited, and pure love that can flow through you into the lives of your wife, your children, and others.

Are you experiencing a drought in your relationship with your child? Are you thirsty for something more in your marriage? Don't rely on yourself. The Master is the only oasis that will ultimately satisfy you and bring pure "living water" back into your relationships. He is the only source of true happiness. And as you empty yourself and constantly tap into Him through continual prayer, reading of His Word, and regular worship at a Bible-based church, your capacity to love and, in turn, lead will not only grow but also will overflow into the lives of your wife and kids.

God is the perfect Father. The better you know Him, the more you will understand how He fathers you with an unfailing love; and the more like Him you become, the better you'll be as a father to your children. As a result, you'll be able to love and lead your children as you convey to them: the immeasurable value they have in their Makeup; the importance of their Mind-set as they grow into young men and women; the underlying Motive of their hearts; the Method to love the unlovable; the way to Model a consistent life of integrity, humility, empathy, and courage; the meaning behind their Message; and, of course, the Source of it all—the Master.

HUDDLE UP AND ASK YOUR CHILD:

1 Do you think God wants a relationship with you? Why?

2 Do you think I do a good job teaching you about God? What is one thing I can do better?

3 How can we make God first in our family?

CONCLUSION
Striving for the Summit

*Every day you may make progress. Every
step may be fruitful. Yet there will stretch
out before you an ever-lengthening, ever-
ascending, ever-improving path. You know
you will never get to the end of the journey.
But this, so far from discouraging, only
adds to the joy and glory of the climb.*

—Sir Winston Churchill

As we started our journey together, I shared with you that I wanted to bring you to a point where you can clearly *see* the summit. Notice I never said that you would actually *reach* the summit. Hopefully you can now see the peak. But you'll never really "arrive" because you should always be striving to be an All Pro Dad. There are still unexplored trails ahead as you reach for the peak, but I'm trusting that I've accomplished what I set out to do.

During our trek we've walked side by side as we've explored our hearts, our minds, and the depths of our souls. Along the way, perhaps you've discovered some valuable things you didn't know. Or maybe some new light was shed upon what you already knew and awakened your desire to push forward as a father. Maybe you even experienced the satisfaction of slaying some of those beasts that had previously wounded you on your journey.

As you peer at the peak of fatherhood, I hope you'll always see it through the lens of love—true love that is strong, powerful, and courageous; true love that is serving, selfless, and sacrificial. As your guide who has been by your side throughout this journey, I trust that I've given you a clear understanding that you must be forever expanding your capacity to love in order to expand your capacity to lead in your home.

You should also now know well the 7 Ms that enable you to execute those fundamentals of love and leadership—Makeup, Mind-set, Motive, Method, Model, Message, and Master.

When you know the 7 Ms and execute the fundamentals of love and leadership with great humility and fierce resolve, you'll leave behind a well-marked trail—a legacy—for your children, grandchildren, and future generations to follow.

Remember playing *Monopoly* when you were a kid? You bought properties like Boardwalk and Park Place. Then, mom said it was time for dinner, and the game was over. Your money, railroads, hotels, and houses were gone. You know, life is like that. You spend years "playing the game" and acquiring "stuff"; then one day your life is over. Your greatest legacy won't be the material things you leave behind; those will fade away. It will be the lives you've touched and the relationships you've built with your wife, your children, and your grandchildren. That legacy will endure even after the game ends.

The dictionary defines a legacy as "something handed down from one who has gone before."[1] I am so grateful that my dad and mom are the ones who have gone before me. It has been the ultimate honor to be their son. I cherish the influence they have had upon my life, and I love them more than they could ever imagine. I previously shared with you about my dad, so I'd like to tell you something very important about my mom as well. When I think of the word *love*, I think of my mom. She is a conduit of God's love. Her life is about giving—giving selflessly and sacrificially to our entire family and to so many others. Other than God Himself, there has been no greater instructor on love in my life than my mom. This book is a part of her legacy.

As Tony Dungy reflected on why our legacies are so important, he said, "As a father, whether you're entrusted with one child or ten, you really shape their life more than anything else, you direct the child from a very, very early stage, and then that life goes on to shape others. And so, you're going to have a whole lineage of family that comes behind you whose attitudes and lives are shaped by decisions that you made."[2] Buccaneers general manager Mark Dominik affirmed Tony's thinking: "Being a dad is my most important job because it not only affects my children, but their children and many generations to come."[3]

Have you thought about your legacy lately? Fathers, we will eventually be that "one who has gone before." How we live will influence our children and descendants for generations. Let me share two stories with you that demonstrate the powerful legacy, both good and bad, that fathers create.

Jonathan Edwards was born in 1703 in East Windsor, Connecticut. He attended Yale University at age thirteen and later went on to serve as president of the College of New Jersey, now Princeton. When he was just twenty years old, he wrote a list of personal resolutions. Among them was to "ask myself, at the end of every day . . . [if] I could possibly, in any respect, have done better."

In no area was Edwards's resolve stronger than in his role as a father. Edwards and his wife, Sarah, had eleven children. Despite a rigorous work schedule that included rising as early as 4:30 a.m. to read and write in his library, extensive travels, and endless meetings, he always made time for his children. Indeed, he committed to spending at least one hour a day with them. And when he missed a day because he was traveling, he diligently made up the hour when he returned.

Numerous books have been written about Edwards's life, his work, and his influence on American history and his powerful professional legacy. But the legacy that Edwards would probably be most proud of is his legacy as a father.

The scholar Benjamin B. Warfield of Princeton charted 1,394 known descendants of Edwards. What he found was an incredible testament to Jonathan Edwards. Of his known descendants there were 13 college presidents, 65 college professors, 30 judges, 100 lawyers, 60 authors, 60 physicians, 75 army and navy officers, 100 pastors, 3 United States senators, 80 public servants in other capacities including governors and ministers to foreign countries, and 1 vice president of the United States.[4]

The story of Jonathan Edwards is an example of what some sociologists call the "five-generation rule." How parents raise their child—the love they give, the values they teach, the emotional environment they offer, the training they provide—influences not only their child but the four generations to follow. In other words, what fathers do in their time will reach through the next five generations. The example of Jonathan Edwards shows just how rich that legacy can be.

But the five-generation rule works both ways. If we fail to work at being good fathers, our neglect can plague generations. Consider the case of Max Jukes, a contemporary of Edwards. As an adult, Jukes had a drinking problem that kept him from holding a steady job. It also kept him from showing much concern for his wife and children. He would disappear sometimes for days and return drunk. He made little time for loving and instructing his children.

Benjamin Warfield also charted Jukes's descendants. His findings further support the five-generation rule. Warfield was able to trace 540 of Jukes's ancestors. They offer a stunning contrast to Edwards's legacy. Of Jukes's known descendants, 310 died as paupers; at least 150 were criminals, including 7 murderers; more than 100 were drunkards; and half of his female descendants ended up as prostitutes.[5]

Of course, this doesn't mean that people are simply a product of their parenting and that who they are is determined entirely by their ancestry. There have been many who descended from men like Jukes and overcame great obstacles to succeed. Others have come from loving homes like Edwards's only to descend into a troubled adulthood. But these are the exceptions, not the rule.

Conclusion

The stories of Jonathan Edwards and Max Jukes offer powerful lessons about the legacy we will leave as fathers. Five generations from now, it is likely that our professional accomplishments will be forgotten. In fact, our descendants may know little about us or our lives. But the way we parent today will directly affect not only our children but also our grandchildren, our great-grandchildren, and the generations that follow.

We will leave a legacy. What will yours be?

ACKNOWLEDGMENTS

How can I adequately express my gratitude to all those who have contributed to this book? I can't. This work is the sum of my life journey as a father, husband, son, brother, and friend. Countless people have positively influenced my life and, therefore, have influenced the words penned on these pages. To all of you, I say a big "thanks!"

Having said that, let me share the names of some folks who have directly touched this work in a special way. Anyone who knows Susan, my amazing and insightful mate of twenty-three years, knows she pursues life with passion and purpose. Susan has challenged, stretched, and inspired me every step of the way as a husband and father. And, I never realized I would learn so much about fatherhood from my own children, but I have. Megan, Emily, Hannah, Marky, and Grant have taught me how to love them well. To say I'm honored to be their dad is an understatement.

Dad and Mom have unconditionally poured out their love upon me and always stressed the importance of family. My brothers and best friends, Bill and Bob, gave me some excellent tips as I wrote. Bill also spent many hours with his red pen making this a much better read.

Rick and Lesley Bateman are like family. They're our lifelong friends who are always there for our family. Barry Banther has been my confidant and personal coach for more than twenty years. He's been by my wise advisor for just about every major decision I've made in my life.

Coach Tony Dungy has been my teammate since 1997. He's been a faithful friend and has dedicated countless hours working with me to encourage men to become All Pro Dads. Coach Clyde Christensen originally introduced me to Tony. He's been a franchise player on the All Pro Dad team since the beginning.

When I think about faithful men and women, our Family First board of directors comes immediately to mind. They have directed the Family First organization and our All Pro Dad program for the past twenty-one years. Thank you, Cary and Ann Gaylord, Charley and Mary Anne Babcock, Steve and Rose Cahill, Michael and Becki Carmichael, Kendall and Sylvia Spencer, Bryant and Joan Skinner.

Our entire Family First team is an incredible group of men and women who are passionate about serving families.

Acknowledgments

The talented Bryan Davis has eagerly supported me in writing this book. Marlene, my loyal assistant, always brings joy to those whose lives she touches, including mine. Thanks also to Amy Bishop who has skillfully helped with research. Bekah Brinkley and Vicki Grimes have provided needed administrative support. Candace Mincey, Courtney Rohrdanz, Darrin Gray, and George Woods have each provided a helping hand as well.

Bill Eyster, Dave Zillig, Steve Casselli, Dustyn Eudaly, and Todd Gongwer have all been involved in reviewing portions of the book manuscript and have given me valuable input.

D. J. Snell has been not only my literary agent, but also a guide by my side in navigating me from the concept of this book to the finished product you are holding in your hands.

Working with Thomas Nelson has been a great experience. So to Joel Miller, Janene MacIvor, Kristi Henson, Jason Jones, and Katy Boatman, I salute you and the rest of the Thomas Nelson team for your service to me and to the men and women whose lives are hopefully changed for the better by the truths in this book.

APPENDIX

Additional Suggestions for the Seven Essentials

MAKEUP

Game Plan: Help your child grow in his or her gifts.

- *Observe* what your child is attracted to. What does your child do well? For example, your child may be mechanically inclined, musically focused, or have excellent hand-eye coordination.
- *Ask* your child, "What are you really good at?" Ask your child's mother, "What is our child's greatest strength?"
- *Tell* your child what you see as his or her greatest gifts.

- *Validate* your child's giftings. Regularly affirm your child's gifts and new ones as they emerge. Discuss how your child's gifts can be used for good.
- *Grow.* Helping your child to grow his or her gifts takes action. If your child displays musical talent, take them to watch a concert pianist. If your child has great hand-eye coordination, watch a tennis match together. If a curiosity of nature is your child's thing, read a book about plants and animals, watch a nature documentary, and take your child on a hike or go camping.

MIND-SET

Game Plan: Get promoted in your most important job.

- *Train.* Read as many good fathering books as you can. Attend fatherhood events with your children. Check out AllProDad.com and find out how to start or join an All Pro Dad's Day at your child's school. Seek the parenting advice of a wise father you admire.
- *Be creative.* Be innovative in things you do with and for your children. It doesn't have to cost much. You could start with the great outdoors. Camping, fishing, and hiking can be wonderful experiences. Throwing the ball in the backyard, building a fort together, going on a picnic, or cooking your child's favorite recipe at home will put a smile on your child's face and build memories.

- *Be honest and reliable.* Honesty always wins. You should be honest with your child at all times, even when it's painful. You should be reliable and keep your word. When you commit to doing something with your child, put it on your calendar and flag it as an important appointment. Never cancel or reschedule unless it is absolutely necessary and make sure you show up on time.
- *Communicate.* Periodically ask your child questions such as, "How am I doing as a dad?" and "What can I do better as a father?" Ask your child's mother the same questions, then take note of their suggestions.
- *Be loyal.* Loyalty means that you walk with your child through the good times and the difficult times. Never give up on your child no matter what your child does or says. Remember that being a dad is a lifetime commitment.

MOTIVE

Game Plan: Check your motives before you make decisions.

- *Ask yourself* if this decision is really best for your child long term or if it is a short-term fix that is convenient for you.
- *Consider* whether this activity is something your child will enjoy or just something you'd like to do.

- *Evaluate* whether making this decision will make you more or less available to your child.
- *Think through* whether this decision will help build your relationship with your child's mother or tear it down.
- *Consider* how this decision will affect your other children. Ask yourself if you are showing favoritism.

METHOD

Game Plan: Build memorable monuments with and for your child.

- *Find your child's favorite thing.* Discover what your child most likes to do with you and then do that together on a weekly or monthly basis. Your child's favorite thing may be photography, working on engines, jogging, biking, cooking, gardening, or attending movies. Ask, and then act on it.
- *Take adventures.* Enjoy the great outdoors with your child. Camping, hunting, canoeing, river rafting, and photography safaris all create lasting memories. Outings to the aquarium, space center, kids' museum, your state or the nation's capital also make great adventures.
- *Establish traditions.* Do things that your child can pass down to their children. For example, at Thanksgiving dinner ask each family member to say what or who

they are thankful for and why. On Mother's Day, make it a tradition for you and your child to buy a present for Mom and then prepare a special meal for her. Each Fourth of July, read the Declaration of Independence and have a barbeque and games in the backyard.

- *Conduct video interviews.* On camera, ask your child open-ended questions that capture who they are, what they are thinking, and what they like to do. These interviews will be priceless heirlooms for generations.
- *Revisit your childhood.* Take your child to the house you grew up in, the school you attended, and the Little League field you played on. Give your child a sense of who you were at his or her age and talk about the joys and challenges of growing up.

MODEL

Game Plan: Be a good role model for your child.

- *Model consistency.* Whether you are with your family, friends, or coworkers, your child needs to see that you are the same person wherever you are and whoever you are with. Your child needs to know that you are the real deal and rock solid, not a person whose personality is constantly shifting.
- *Model self-denial.* It's easy to live a life that's focused on "me." Your child needs to see that you're willing to

forego buying things and doing things that would give you comfort and pleasure.

- *Model honor.* If you want your child to honor and respect you, then show your child how it's done. Honor your mother and father, whether you think they deserve it or not.

- *Model control over words.* Words matter. You need to chain your tongue, tame it, and train it. Make sure the words that come out of your mouth toward your spouse, your child, your friends, and even your enemies are respectful and kind.

- *Model appropriate actions.* Your child is always watching. Your child sees the kinds of movies and television shows you watch, notices the music you listen to, the people you associate with, the way you drive, and the way you treat your spouse and other people. Your child's actions will often be a reflection of your actions. As Benjamin Franklin put it, "Well done is better than well said."

MESSAGE

Game Plan: You and your child should serve others.

- *Serve in your home.* You don't have to look any farther than the four walls of your home to serve others. Doing chores together around the house, like washing dishes, vacuuming, and taking the garbage out, even when it isn't your job, will teach your child how to serve.

- *Serve in your neighborhood.* Do you have a widow living next door? Mow her yard. Is there an overwhelmed single mom or dad nearby? Babysit his or her child for free.

- *Serve in your community.* Most communities have facilities to feed the hungry and house the poor. Offer to help. There are many lonely elderly people in nursing homes who would cherish a visit from you and your child.

- *Serve in your country.* There are people in need all over your state and nation. Children in the foster care system need nurturing families. There are many children awaiting adoption who need a permanent place to lay their heads, be hugged, and be loved. Find a way to show soldiers from your area that you appreciate their sacrifice.

- *Serve in your world.* Many Americans don't understand extreme poverty. There are countries where people are searching for clean water to drink and food to sustain their lives. Perhaps you are able to travel abroad to help those who hurt, or financially support an organization that addresses some of these needs.

Appendix

MASTER

Game Plan: Do not waste your life.

- *Identify a reference point for success.* Set loving God and loving others as your standard for a successful life. Everything you say and do should run through this filter.
- *Value relationships above all else.* Value investing in people above investing in things.
- *Remember the source of your joy and true value.* C. S. Lewis said, "Don't let your happiness depend on something you may lose." If you depend on others or on things to make you happy, or if your self-worth depends on achievements, you undermine your reason for being. Your joy should come from knowing who you are and whose you are.
- *Pursue long-term rewards.* Many people sacrifice long-term joy, satisfaction, and contentment for short-term personal pleasures. Things like drugs, pornography, and gambling will never satisfy. What will satisfy is living a life of meaning and purpose—a life that honors the Master.
- *Remember you are always in God's presence.* Never do anything you wouldn't be comfortable doing in the presence of the Master. He knows all, sees all, and is all-powerful. He also cares for you and loves you more than you'll ever know.

NOTES

Chapter 1

1. Author interview with Tony Dungy, September 27, 2010, and July 29, 2011.

2. Author interview with James "JB" Brown, August 17, 2010.

3. G. K. Chesterton, *Illustrated London News*, January 14, 1911.

4. Rick Reilly, "John Wooden Love Letters" ESPN Video, http://www.youtube.com/watch?v=tySxPue9Dmw.

5. Jack Canfield, Mark Victor Hansen, Maida Rogerson, Martin Ruete, and Tim Clauss, *Chicken Soup for the Soul at Work: 101 Stories of Courage, Compassion & Creativity in the Workplace* (Deerfield Beach, Health Communications, Inc., 1996), 23.

6. Jack Canfield, Mark Victor Hansen, Hanoch McCarty, and Meladee McCarty, *A 4th Course of Chicken Soup for the Soul: 101 Stories to Open the Heart and Rekindle the Spirit* (Deerfield Beach, Health Communications, Inc., 1997), 204.

7. Mahatma Gandhi, *All Men Are Brothers: Autobiographical Reflections* (New York, The Continuum International Publishing Group Inc., 2004), 65.

8. Matthew 22:36–39.

9. C. S. Lewis, *The Four Loves* (New York: Harcourt Brace Jovanovich, 1960), 121.

10. 1 Corinthians 13:4–7.

11. Author interview with Michael W. Smith, July 26, 2011.

12. Author interview with Jeb Bush, August 19, 2010.

13. Author interview with Jim Caldwell, May 14, 2010.

14. Author interview with J. Wayne Huizenga Jr., August 16, 2010.

15. Phil Dourado, *The 60 Second Leader* (UK: Capstone Publishing, LTD., 2007), 158.

16. Author interview with James "JB" Brown, August 17, 2010.

17. Author interview with Michael Ducker, August 17, 2010.

18. Author interview with Tony Dungy, September 27, 2010, and July 29, 2011.

Chapter 2

1. Wade F. Horn, Ph.D. and Tom Sylvester, *Father Facts*, Fourth Edition (Gaithersburg, MD: National Fatherhood Initiative, 2002), 23.

2. "Fatherless Florida II: A Survey of Juvenile Offenders," February 26, 1997, a survey of juvenile offenders in Florida state institutions.

3. "TV, Internet and Mobile Usage in U.S. Continues to Rise," nielsenwire.com, February 23, 2009.

4. Gretchen Livingston and Kim Parker, "A Tale of Two Fathers," Pew Research Center, *Pew Social & Demographic Trends*, June 15, 2011.

5. Offbeat, "450 sheep jump to their deaths in Turkey," USA Today .com, July 9, 2005.

6. *What a Girl Wants* (2003).

7. Author interview with Tony Dungy, September 27, 2010, and July 29, 2011.

8. AP, "Art experts find possible new da Vinci," Long Island Press .com, October 14, 2009. http://www.longislandpress.com/2009/10/14/art-experts-find-possible-new-da-vinci/.

9. Author interview with Dr. Ben Carson, October 14, 2010.

10. Author interview with S. Truett Cathy, October 4, 2010.

11. Jack Canfield, Mark Victor Hansen, and Amy Newmark, *Chicken Soup for the Soul, Just for Preteens* (Cos Cob, CT: Chicken Soup for the Soul Publishing, LLC, 2011), 2.

12. Gretchen Rubin, *Forty Ways to Look at Winston Churchill: A Brief Account of a Long Life* (New York: Random House, 2004), 61–62.

13. Author interview with Jeb Bush, August 19, 2010.

Chapter 3

1. Devin G. Pope and Maurice E. Schweitzer, "Is Tiger Woods Loss Averse? Persistent Bias in the Face of Experience, Competition, and High Stakes," *American Economic Review*, 101(1): 129–57.

2. Jeffrey Marx, *Season of Life* (New York: Simon & Schuster, 2003), 36.

3. Navy SEALs: Special Operations: Careers & Jobs: Navy.com and Navy SEALs Frequently Asked Questions, SEALSWCC.com.

4. Nick Carbone, "Inside Navy SEAL Team 6," Time.com, May 10, 2011.

5. Nicholas Schmidle, "Getting Bin Laden," New Yorker.com, August 8, 2011.

6. Francis Chan, *Crazy Love* (Colorado Springs: David C. Cook, 2008), 93.

7. Author interview with Norm Miller, August 17, 2010.

8. Stephen Kendrick and Alex Kendrick, *The Love Dare* (Nashville: B & H Publishing Group, 2008), 6.

9. Jack Canfield and Mark Victor Hansen, *A 3rd Serving of Chicken Soup for the Soul* (Deerfield Beach, FL: Health Communication, Inc., 1996), 12.

10. Rick Warren, *40 Days of Love Video Study Guide* (Grand Rapids: Zondervan, 2009), 108 (author's emphasis).

11. Jeffrey Dew, "Bank On It: Thrifty Couples Are the Happiest," *State of Our Unions* (2009), 3 and Fig. 3. http://stateofourunions .org/2009/bank_on_it.php.

12. Dave Ramsey, "The Seven Baby Steps," (steps 1–3), accessed February 14, 2012, http://www.daveramsey.com/new/baby-steps/.

Chapter 4

1. Kendrick, *The Love Dare*, 211.

2. Ibid., 212.

3. Matthew 6:21.

4. Proverbs 4:23.

5. Author interview with Michael W. Smith, July 26, 2011.

6. "The United States Population in International Context: 2000," nationalatlas.gov.

7. Terence Monmaney, "George Friedman on World War III," Smithsonian.com, August 2010.

8. Stephen Mansfield, *Never Give In: The Extraordinary Character of Winston Churchill* (Nashville: Cumberland House Publishing, 1995), 224.

9. Author interview with Tony Dungy, September 27, 2010, and July 29, 2011.

10. Author interview with Norm Miller, August 17, 2010.

Chapter 5

1. NatureWorks, "North American Porcupine," nhptv.org.

2. Author interview with Mark Dominik, July 27, 2010.

3. John 14:15.

4. Psalm 1:1–3.

5. Erma Bombeck, *Forever, Erma* (Kansas City: Andrews McMeel Publishing, LLC, 1997), 13.

Chapter 6

1. Matthew 15:18 ESV.

2. Author interview with Michael Ducker, August 17, 2010.

3. Author interview with J. Wayne Huizenga Jr., August 16, 2010.

4. Author interview with Dan Cathy, August 26, 2010.

5. Max Lucado, *He Still Moves Stones* (Nashville: Thomas Nelson, 1999), 68.

6. Archibald Henderson, *Mark Twain* (UK: The Echo Library, 2008), 50.

7. Charles Barkley, "I am not a role model." Nike Air commercial, YouTube, accessed February 14, 2012, http://www.youtube.com/watch?v=R8vh2MwXZ6o.

8. Jim Collins, *Good to Great* (New York: HarperCollins, 2001), 21.

9. Max Lucado, *Traveling Light* (Nashville: Thomas Nelson, 2001), 75–76.

10. Author interview with Michael W. Smith, July 26, 2011.

11. Author interview with Tony Dungy, September 27, 2010, and July 29, 2011.

12. Author interview with Jim Caldwell, May 14, 2010.

13. Author interview with Tony Dungy, September 27, 2010, and July 29, 2011.

Chapter 7

1. Rick Warren, *The Purpose Driven Life* (Grand Rapids: Zondervan, 2002), 33.

2. *Chariots of Fire* (1981) and Bill Mallon and Jeroen Heijmans, *Historical Dictionary of the Olympic Movement* (Lanham: Scarecrow Press, Inc., 2011), xlvii, 75.

3. Author interview with S. Truett Cathy, October 4, 2010.

4. Fr. Andrew C. Smith Jr. (Fr. Drew), *From the Gun to the Pulpit* (USA, 2010), 105.

5. Barbara Johnson, *Christian Acts of Kindness* (Berkeley, CA: Grace House, 1999), 128.

Chapter 8

1. Author interview with Barry Banther, May 24, 2010.

2. Author interview with Jude Thompson, August 12, 2010.

3. Author interview with Dave Dunkel, May 18, 2010.

4. Author interview with Mark Richt, August 16, 2010.

5. Joe Gibbs, *Game Plan for Life* (Carol Stream, Illinois: Tyndale House Publishers, Inc., 2009), 175–76.

6. Author interview with Dr. Ben Carson, October 14, 2010.

7. Susie O'Berski, *We Are the Much More* (USA: Xulonpress, 2010), 135.

8. Author interview with Dr. Ben Carson, October 14, 2010.

9. Tongass National Forest, "The Salmon Life Cycle," *U.S. Forest Service*, http://www.fs.fed.us/r10/tongass/districts/mendenhall/fishcam/lifecycle.shtml and *Fish Ex Quality Seafoods*, "The Fascinating Life of an Alaskan Salmon," fishex.com. http://www.fishex.com/seafood/salmon/salmon-life-cycles.html.

10. C. S. Lewis, *Mere Christianity* (Nashville: Broadman & Holman Publishers, 1952), 30.

11. Ibid., 121.

12. Josh McDowell, *The New Evidence That Demands A Verdict* (Nashville: Thomas Nelson, 1999), 4–7.

13. Lee Strobel, *The Case for Christ* (Grand Rapids: Zondervan, 1998), 60, 63. McDowell, *The New Evidence*, 38.

14. Assayas, Michka, *Bono* (New York: The Berkley Publishing Group, 2005), 226–27.

15. C. S. Lewis, *Mere Christianity* (Nashville: Broadman & Holman Publishers, 1952), 54.

16. Todd G. Gongwer, *Lead . . . for God's Sake!* (Nappanee, IN: Evangel Press, 2010), 132.

Conclusion

1. *Webster's II New Riverside Desk Dictionary* (Boston: Houghton Mifflin, 1988), 241.

2. Author interview with Tony Dungy, September 27, 2010, and July 29, 2011.

3. Author interview with Mark Dominik, July 27, 2010.

4. Roy B. Zuck, *The Speaker's Quote Book* (Grand Rapids: Kregel Publications, 2009), 277.

5. Ibid.

ABOUT THE AUTHOR

Mark Merrill is the founder and president of Family First, a national non-profit organization dedicated to strengthening the family. Mark hosts the *Family Minute with Mark Merrill*, a nationally syndicated daily radio program. He has appeared on NBC's *Today Show*, numerous ABC, CBS, FOX, and NBC network affiliates and national radio programs. His comments and writings have appeared in publications including *USA Today*, the *Washington Times*, and *Sports Illustrated*. As an energetic advocate for the family, Mark speaks at conferences and events hosted by major companies and organizations and NFL teams, as well as special engagements for dignitaries. Before founding Family First in 1991, Mark practiced law in Florida for seven years. Mark and his wife, Susan, live in Tampa, Florida, and have five children.

About the Author

For more about the book visit AllProDadBook.com.
Follow Mark and All Pro Dad on Twitter @
MarkMerrill@AllProDad.
Like them at Facebook: /MarkMerrill/AllProDad.
To connect with Mark visit MarkMerrill.com,
Facebook.com/MarkMerrill, and Twitter.com/MarkMerrill.

Meet Mark Merrill

Radio Host.

The *Family Minute with Mark Merrill* is a nationally syndicated radio feature that reaches millions each weekday on hundreds of radio stations, SIRIUS XM Satellite Radio, and the American Forces Network worldwide. To listen to the Family Minute online, or to find a radio station near you, go to FamilyMinute.com.

Speaker.

Mark touches thousands of lives as he speaks at conferences and events hosted by major companies and organizations, NFL teams, as well as special engagements for dignitaries. Mark is passionate about speaking on topics such as parenting, fatherhood, marriage, and leadership. To schedule Mark to speak for your event, visit MarkMerrill.com.

Blogger.

Social media gives Mark another way to further extend his connection to families all around the world. Since launching his social media efforts in 2010, he now has hundreds of thousands of connections on Twitter, Facebook, and his blog.

Connect with Mark Today.

Visit MarkMerrill.com.

NOTE FROM THE AUTHOR'S WIFE

I'm so encouraged that you've completed this book. I hope you've caught a vision for what it looks like to be an All Pro Dad. As Mark said, "You'll never really 'arrive' because you should always be striving to be an All Pro Dad."

Mark is still striving to be an All Pro Dad too. In fact, Mark and I are wrapping up a season of raising five teenagers. I say that to let you know that my husband wrote this book in complete humility. As a father and husband, Mark has felt the joy of victory when he has done his job well, and the pain of failure when he hasn't. But this one thing I do know. Mark always perseveres and pursues being the best loving leader in our home that he can be.

I want to encourage you to persevere as well. Be the best you can be today. The rewards you experience as a husband and dad may come quickly or they may come many years from now. But don't give up! The legacy of love you leave your children will be worth it. Your legacy will not only impact your children but generations to come.

—Susan Merrill,
Director of iMom

What is iMOM?

iMOM is a program that all moms can count on to help them be the best moms they can be. The program provides information, ideas, inspiration and insight to mothers through its resource rich website, iMOM.com, its thought-provoking daily email, *The Espresso Minute*, and its school-based program for moms and kids, iMOM Morning. With national Ambassadors like Denise Jonas and Lauren Dungy, iMOM speaks to the hearts of moms across the U.S. and around the world.

To find out more about us and our events, visit iMOM.com today.

WHAT IS ALL PRO DAD?

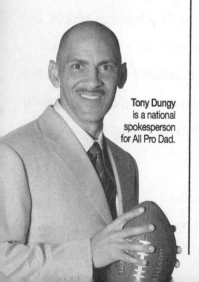

Tony Dungy is a national spokesperson for All Pro Dad.

All Pro Dad reaches hundreds of thousands of men every day with practical parenting advice. All Pro Dad features NFL coaches, players, and alumni who speak out about the importance of fatherhood. Through its website, as well as the *Play of the Day* Email, the All Pro Dad's Day School Breakfast program, and national NFL events, All Pro Dad gives men the tools they need to be better fathers.

To find out more about us and our events visit AllProDad.com today.

ALL PRO DAD